REJUVENATING A GARDEN

Rejuvenating

a Garden

Stephen Anderton

The publishers would like to thank
THE GARDEN PICTURE LIBRARY
Unit 12 Ransome's Dock • 35 Parkgate Road • London • SW11 4NP
tel: +44 (0) 207 228 4332 • fax: +44 (0) 207 924 3267
for their kind assistance in the production of this book.

First published in hardback in Great Britain, 1998 by
Kyle Cathie Limited
122 Arlington Road
London NW1 7HP

First published in paperback in 2001

2 4 6 8 10 9 7 5 3 1

ISBN 1 85626 435 1

Text © 1998 Stephen Anderton
Photography © 1998 Stephen Anderton, Nic Barlow,
Michelle Garrett, Hugh Palmer

Stephen Anderton is hereby identified as the author of this work in accordance with
Section 77 of the Copyright, Designs and Patents Act 1988

A Cataloguing In Publication record for this title is available from the British Library.

Editor: Kate Oldfield
Copy editor: Penny David
Design: Robert Updegraff
Production: Lorraine Baird

Colour separation by Colourscan Overseas Co. Pte. Ltd.
Typeset: R & B Creative Services
Printed and bound in Singapore through Tien Wah Press Pte. Ltd.

for Judith, Eleanor, Rosamund and Olivia

CONTENTS

Introduction

If ever you have gone out into a new garden and thought "Where on earth do I start?", then this book is intended for you. It can be a daunting feeling to have to tackle a neglected garden, or even a part of one. Fortunately, the muddle is rarely as bad as it seems, and with a logical approach and a knowledge of what you can get away with, order usually rises from the chaos.

Even gardens which are well maintained need new life breathed into them every 20–30 years. They become stale and old like anything else, and can be much in need of a sharp axe and a hard heart. The secret of success in rejuvenating a garden, as this book will show, is in knowing when and where to apply the axe, and which plants will respond to heavy cutting. It is so helpful to know when to be cruel to be kind – and when to be kind to be kind. Hearts can be harder to sharpen than axes, but they soon get into the swing of it.

There is nothing more exciting than seeing an old, congested garden or shrubbery given room to breathe once more, and to see solid, overgrown plantings give way to light and space. The remaining plants heave a sigh, and smile and learn to live life to the full again. Health returns, and flower, and perfume, and light and shade.

Gardens are composed of many interlocking elements, each with a different life span. There may be trees capable of living anywhere between 70 and 300 years, and shrubs whose life span may vary from 5–100 years. There may be walls and paving needing attention every 10–20 years. There will be the perennial and annual flowers, the soft furnishings and adornments of a garden, which will need changing every few years or months.

But change they must. And adapt they must. With all these interlocking cycles of decay, a garden is forever changing. Left to itself any garden will return in a few short years to a glorious jungle, in which only the fittest survive. As gardeners, it is our perpetual pleasure to adjust that progress to suit our eyes, making sure that the plants we prefer survive, and not just the Japanese knotweed.

With luck and good management we can plan so that all this change happens at the best speed for the garden, keeping old plants where required, but not being afraid to rip them out when necessary, so that the garden never reaches that terminal condition when all those cycles of decay grind to a barren halt together.

Badly neglected gardens are difficult to handle, because there is so much needing attention all at once. Emergency injections are needed, of time and energy and sometimes money. The only way to proceed is to prioritise the work, not feeling you have to tackle everything at once, but doing first those things which matter most to the health and life of the garden, and those which matter most to you as the person who has to live in it.

It may be that you have grand plans to alter the garden to suit your requirements. You may want to redesign the garden simply for the pleasure and fun of remaking it. You may need to adapt a densely-planted, high-maintenance garden to survive on an hour a week without looking a mess. Few serious gardeners have as much time to garden as they would like, and some people quite rightly want to do completely different things with their free time. Sky diving can be almost as fascinating as gardening, after all. It may be you want to move the other way, and to find suitable positions in a bald and empty garden for a whole range of new plants, in shade and sun, or perhaps a specialised collection of hellebores or cannas. Perhaps you only want some terrace pots, a couple of trees, and a lawn where the children can run around.

Whatever you want to do with the garden, there are two ways to proceed. You can scrap the whole thing and start again from a clean sheet. It is expensive and drastic. Or you can keep the best of the previous garden, and build upon that. Unless you are burning to implement plans for a new designer garden which will brook no compromise, then it is usually better to proceed by building on the past. If you can manage to retain old garden features and old plants, then the garden will have access to a dignity and sense of establishment which comes only with the passage of time and can rarely be bought. At the same time you will keep your options on shade, shelter and privacy.

Rejuvenating a garden is rather like repairing a house. Once the structural problems are solved, there is then time to enjoy creating the colour schemes and the details of its furnishing and decoration. There is time to enjoy simply being in the garden, and the pleasures of growing plants. Maintaining a garden (as opposed to designing one) has been called 'a performance art within a semi-permanent framework'. This book is there to help you sort out an efficient and healthy framework, so you then have time to enjoy the classic role of gardener. Gardening should be all greasepaint and roses.

PART I Where to Start

Assessing the soil and climate

Assessing the plants

Assessing the structure

Assessing the restrictions

Understanding your own needs

Understanding your gardening needs

Rustic paving to solve the problem of hot, dry, stony, rooty soil in shade? Grass instead would emphasise the vista, but would it grow here?

Assessing Soil and Climate

In starting work on any garden, the greatest tools you have are your imagination, muscle power and the soil itself. So an hour spent in looking at how things are growing and in doing a bit of exploratory digging will never be wasted. Knowing just what is down there will stop you making unrealistic plans later.

Most of us never have the nerve or opportunity to find out about the soil before we move into a house. It is usually a matter of trusting to general impressions and discovering the reality of sand, clay or rich loam after we move in. Most estate agents do not take kindly to prospective buyers turning up to view a house with a spade under one arm, but a quick look at the soil can tell you so much.

Fertility symbols

Even without digging, it is worth looking hard at the plants in a new or prospective garden, to assess what the soil might be like. Soil fertility is not the easiest thing to gauge. Ornamental perennials usually require more frequent replanting and feeding than native plants and miserable congested perennials do not

necessarily mean the soil is poor, only that the garden has not been seriously cultivated for a long time.

Turf and tree vigour

It is better to look at the trees and the grass to learn about the soil. Are the trees making strong vigorous growth? Is their canopy thin and foliage sparse for the time of year? If the grass has not been cut for months, is it lush and tall from a rich diet and has it fallen over under its own abundant weight? Or is it sparse, short, and lean enough not to flop over, suggesting a poor or stony soil?

Acid or alkaline?

Look at the range of plants to see if there are any lime-haters there, such as rhododendrons, pieris and summer-flowering heathers. If there are, and if they are planted in the ground rather than in raised beds, then the soil must have a neutral or acidic pH level. If there are no lime-hating plants at all, then it is reasonable to suspect that the soil is alkaline. A few tests made with a kit from the garden centre will give a clearer picture. It is also worth glancing at neighbouring gardens, to see if there are any acid-loving plants in the district.

Sun scorch on golden philadelphus (left).
Rhododendron flowers spoiled by frost (right).

Moisture

Look at the drainage, especially in the lower areas of the garden. Is it boggy, even in summer? Are there standing dead trees in the wet areas, which may have died from waterlogging? If so, could *that* be used to advantage for moisture-loving plants? Or would you need to put in new drains to accommodate your plans?

Find out the local annual rainfall figure. Local horticultural societies or the Environment Agency will be able to help you there. If the soil is dry and thin, then low rainfall and drought are going to be significant factors in your choice of plants.

Frost pockets

Consider whether the garden might be a frost pocket. Look for signs of frost damage in the leaders and branches on trees: they may be kinked where the leading shoot has been regularly killed back and a side shoot has taken over. Look for congested growth in the canopy of shrubs, where late spring frosts have cut back the emerging shoots and encouraged the proliferation of smaller replacement shoots later in the season.

If the frost pocket is at the bottom of a hill, there is little you can do about it. You will need to concentrate on planting tough species and preferably those which do not come into leaf early. Often, however, frost pockets on a slope can be 'drained', by opening up the planting through pruning and thinning, so that cold air currents fall away to lower levels.

Exposure

The condition of the plants can tell you a great deal about how exposed to wind a garden may be. Look at what protection there is from the likely prevailing winds. Are shelter trees wind-shaped, with short branches on the windward side and longer ones on the lee side? Are plants against walls thrust forward by buffeting winds striking off the wall behind them? Are evergreens wind-burned? Does the apparent calmness depend on the present jungle of overgrowth?

TEST HOLES

Where there is space, dig a few test holes to look at the soil. Try to get down at least 60–90cm (2–3ft) so that you have a good idea of what is down there. Take note of whether you

Digging a test hole to discover what your soil consists of.

reach gravel, clay, sand or chalk, or whether the soil is full of flints or large stones or even builders' rubble. What you find in one hole will not necessarily be what you find in another, so do not be too disheartened if you strike rubble or chalk at the outset. Try a few different places around the garden and make a general assessment of what is in store for you. To save work, take the opportunity of digging out any properly dead shrubs to make your test holes.

Soil tests are quick, simple and cheap, so do several to give you a good indication of the state of your soil.

Assessing the Plants

A garden that has been well cared for throughout its life will coast very happily into middle age. Everyone longs for one of those. On the other hand, a garden that has had only poor care and little long-term thought will present a very different picture, of crowding and disease. Before you make your own new plans for the garden, you need to sort out what the prospects are for the plants in the garden as it stands. Take a look first at which plants are thriving and which are suffering. A hard look at the way different plants are performing will often highlight the garden's most pressing problems.

Which plants are performing badly?

The commonest problem is lack of light from unchecked trees, causing a weary, starved-looking shrub and herbaceous storey beneath. Unless you want to move to woodland-floor gardening only, some hard decisions will have to be made about which trees and shrubs to take out. With their removal, you will be able to open up and enrich new areas of vacant soil. Here the competition from surface roots will be less fierce and much more suitable for new planting. In increased light most evergreens and conifers will thicken up once more, shrubs will cease, after pruning, to be leggy and drawn and herbaceous plants will flower properly again.

In more open gardens, the problem may be the sheer volume of unchecked growth made by shrubs and an invasion of weeds. By pruning long-lived shrubs and removing or replacing overgrown short-term shrubs, you will open the road to recovery. Mechanical and chemical weed control will start the slower progress to a garden free of weeds.

Which plants are doing too well?

Sometimes a garden fills up with vigorous exotic weeds which at first glance might be thought to be an intentional planting. Leycesteria, buddleja, brooms, cotoneaster, hypericums and berberis all have a habit of seeding or suckering around and quickly making sizeable plants. Watch out for opportunists such as these smothering more valuable plants. Do not be afraid to pull them out wholesale if they are serving no useful purpose.

Overgrown lawns are not a problem. Simply get them cut down, with a hired heavy mower if necessary and then keep them cut. Serious weed problems such as dock and thistle can be dealt with all in good time, when more pressing matters have been dealt with.

If rough grass stays short in a wet season, then the soil is probably starved, and good for meadow gardening.

How old is the yew arch? It could be 50, 150 or 200 years old.

What is the average age of your plants?

Take a hard look at the various elements of planting in your garden – trees, shrubs, climbers and so on – to decide how far they are into their cycle of growth and decline. Often what looks like one phase of a garden's planting allowed to get into a muddle turns out to be planting from two or three periods, often decades apart and with layers of seedling growth on top.

Take a long look at the trees

Look first at the trees. In a small garden you might have only one youthful 8m (25ft) tree. If you are going to be there for five years, then that is fine. Its smothering, overwhelming maturity will be someone else's problem. But if you are intending to be there for the second half of your life and you are a keen gardener, then you may consider having the tree out now (planning regulations permitting: see page 54) and replacing it with two or three younger ones. Just because trees live to a great age, it does not mean to say they have to do so in your own garden. What is important is always to have young trees coming on, to keep your options open.

Larger gardens, and especially neglected gardens, have a tendency to fill up with trees. If you have inherited a rectangle of 'forest garden', look at the relative ages of the trees. Are they young, middle-aged, or about to give up the ghost any day now? If old, wouldn't you rather have them out now while you are making a mess and be able to plant without risk of subsequent damage? On the other hand you may love their mass and venerability and may settle for the prospect of letting them all go gradually in their own good time. You may wish to keep perhaps just one or two, in one area and to settle for not being able to make any further

substantial planting in that area for the foreseeable future. You could let them depart this world romantically, in a surplice of 'Rambling Rector' or other rampant flowering climbers.

If trees are well spaced but all of one age, you may like to remove one or two to create some diversity of age within the garden. When disaster strikes, in the form of a great storm, it is usually the very old and the very young which succumb to it. If you intend to live there long, there is value in having a spread of age ranges – to have your eggs in more than one basket – so that the trials of nature never take the garden back to square one, with all the trees dying together. Call this a counsel of perfection if you will, but age diversity has other advantages. It allows you to try new trees and to enjoy their youth as much as their age.

Looking at the shrub layer

Assess the state of the shrubs, too. On average, most shrubs have a lifespan of 10–60 years. But size does not necessarily equate with old age. It may well be that after cutting them to the ground, you could, by regular seasonal pruning, get those hydrangeas, mock orange and weigelas back to 2m (6ft) instead of 3m (10ft), and get back your view of the village church with secateurs rather than a spade.

Before you redesign the inner part of your garden, consider whether it depends for privacy and shelter at the edges on shrubs ready to fall over with old age. And are those shrubs ones which will regenerate from hard pruning, such as hybrid rhododendrons and laurels? Or are they species which refuse to respond, like brooms and cypresses?

It may be colourful, but with every passing year the strong plants are now squeezing out the weak. Would that matter to you?

Bracket fungi on large trees usually mean the beginning of the not-too-distant end. Get a professional opinion from a tree surgeon.

Self-sown shrubs and trees can grow at an astonishing speed, outstripping older neighbours and becoming cuckoos in the border after only four or five years. Even in well-tended gardens, seedling shrubs and trees like elder, ash, sycamore and holly slide themselves in, eclipsing more precious plants. Look hard at them all. It may be that the precious daphne or variegated holly is past redemption. In which case the self-sown buddlejas or elder may be the ones to keep for the present. It would be a mean gardener to call any plant which hides a critical vista to a motorway junction a weed. Especially if it flowers as generously as an elder. Think time: do I want a hideous view, or do I want temporary cover to get something better established?

Diagnosing disease

If there are serious diseases present in a garden, the sooner you know about them the better. It will help you plan your planting so as to avoid furthering the problem.

Inspect any wholly dead trees or shrubs and look for any obvious signs of disease. Death may have been just a case of old age, but be suspicious of anything dead which is still holding its brown leaves, of plants dying a branch at a time, of plants that die suddenly during the growing season and of clusters of dead plants in one area of the garden. These are symptoms of honey fungus (species of *Armillaria*), which comes in several forms. One can kill healthy plants outright; another will attack and kill already stressed plants and a third, less dangerous form can leave plants almost unaffected. Simply seeing any of the symptoms of the disease is no cause for panic. Take it as it comes, but be careful and be hygienic.

Look out, too, for plants with bracket fungi either on the base or near old major wounds. These can mean the tree has a fatal infection of the trunk or roots, which could lead to collapse in a few years. The most common forms include *Heterobasidion* on conifers and *Ganoderma*, *Fistulina* and *Inonotus* on broadleaved trees. Get a professional to inspect the tree, before either you plan the garden round it, or it falls over. If needs be, have it made safe or felled.

Phytophthora is another problem disease, killing woody plants suddenly, rather like honey fungus. It likes to run through coniferous hedges, especially on poorly drained soil. Look for dark, discoloured roots and stems. Burn the plant and its roots and replace the soil if practical.

Think hard about badly cankered fruit trees or trees with severe silverleaf or fireblight. Unless you are anxious to keep their presence for a few years longer, as a screen or shelter, it may be better to have them out at the start, while you are making a mess.

More minor diseases such as mildew and rusts need be no cause for concern in an overgrown garden. Forget them for now. Once you have cut back overgrowth and let air and moisture back into the garden, that is the time to consider how to deal with any remaining diseases.

HONEY FUNGUS

This has several diagnostic features, of which you may see all or none. These include a) a white mushroom-smelling mould under the bark at the base of the trunk, b) black, flattened, rather elastic 'bootlaces' under the bark of the trunk or on the surface of major roots, and c) clusters of honey-coloured toadstools in late summer or autumn, with a distinct creamy ring or ruff on the stem.

The first and best treatment for honey fungus is good hygiene. Remove dead trees, including especially the stump, so that the fungus is denied the nourishment of its victim. Treat the area with phenolic compounds such as Armillotox, and wait a few years before reintroducing woody plants with some known resistance to the area. Like sci-fi monsters, honey fungus has a habit of coming back just as you thought it was licked.

Ironically, honey fungus is a greater problem in gardens than in natural woodlands where it must compete with other wood-eating fungi.

Plants resistant to honey fungus

Abutilon	*Choisya* (Mexican orange blossom)	*Photinia*
Bamboos	*Cotinus* (smoke tree)	*Pieris*
Buxus (box, boxwood)	*Elaeagnus*	*Quercus* (oak)
Carpenteria	*Fagus* (beech)	*Rhus* (sumach)
Catalpa (Indian bean tree)	*Hebe*	*Sambucus* (elder)
Cercis (Judas tree)	*Ilex* (holly)	*Tamarix* (tamarisk)
Chaenomeles (japonica, flowering quince)	*Kerria* (Jew's mallow)	*Taxus* (yew)

Assessing the Structure

Before you redevelop a garden to your own taste, or even repair it in its present form, it is worth looking hard at the structure that already exists – the paths, steps, walls and open spaces – to read their style and period and to see how the design was originally intended to work. Whatever you want to achieve, the garden needs to complement the house. The house is the biggest piece of structure in any garden and you must work with it, not against it. It is always worth trying to understand how others before you have gardened on the site, so you can appreciate the remaining strengths of the design and incorporate them into your new garden. Scrap them altogether if you like, but be sure you know what you are getting rid of.

Patterns from the past

Usually the first layout of the garden, made when the house was first built, will dominate the garden, setting out the levels and open spaces. A Victorian town house, for instance, would originally have had a formal front garden, screened from the road with evergreen shrubberies, gravel or asphalt paths with rope-tile edges and tightly shaped beds for annual flowers. There may be an island bed in the centre of the space where vehicles turned, or a central path to the front door.

An old garden may also have a succession of later overlays made by subsequent owners – beds to add more colour, hedges or flowering shrubs to subdivide the garden; features may have

Six months' growth would swallow this mossy deity completely.

Old walls can have great charm and dignity. Repair them when practically necessary but not before.

been removed or replaced; vegetable beds may have been grassed down to reduce maintenance. It may be that the garden has never had any serious thought or planning at all and has only a few old apple trees or simply bare grass. There may be just years and years of neglect, with the bigger plants competing for light and any pruning having been done by the 'basin haircut' technique – only cutting off anything which sticks out around the edges.

When you find the logic of what has been done around the house in the past, you can then decide whether it is of use to you and how best to develop the garden next. It is surprising how often a gardener who likes a flowing, natural garden style, when confronted with living in a four-square, visually dominant house, will opt for the logic of a rather more formalized style, simply to match strength with strength. The same person, given an old country cottage, would make a deliciously ramshackle, muddly cottage garden and love it just as much.

Boundaries and barriers

Look at the condition of the structural elements in the garden. Are the walls and steps crumbling or in good order? Do they need repointing or can they be left alone for another 10 years? Maybe so long as they are sound, you would much prefer not to see them repointed and looking like new. Old walls can be stripped of all their character by unsympathetic repointing. Ask your builder to use lime mortar rather than a hard Portland cement mix, if in doubt.

Retaining terrace walls, in particular, need repairing before they fall.

Retaining walls are especially prone to problems in old age, because of the pressure of soil and roots behind them. Repairing or reconstructing them may result in damage to plants above and below. Sometimes it is major roots which are the principal cause of the damage and a hard decision may have to be made about whether to save the plant or the wall. There is no right or wrong answer to this. Enjoy the tree for another 20 years and you will pay the price of more serious and expensive damage to the wall. Give priority to the wall and you lose 20 years' pleasure from the tree. All you can do is make a balanced decision.

Look at the fences, boundaries and gates and check whether they are yours to maintain or a neighbour's. Will paint and preservatives do all that is necessary, or do rotten fence posts need replacing and gates rehanging?

Hedges are part of the structure of a garden and play a vital role in providing shelter, privacy and a sense of place to inner compartments of the garden. But are they unmanageably tall or wide? Do they need some horticultural liposuction – with a

sharp saw – to streamline their figure? Are they on their last legs and likely to die out altogether? Would it be better to replace them early on, while you are making a mess? Perhaps there are too many hedges for your purpose and you could usefully grub some out and save a lot of clipping later?

Watching your step

Is the paving dangerously uneven? Could it be relaid, or does it really need replacing? Are gravel paths riddled with weeds because they have no hard foundation and are laid meanly over soil, or are they well constructed on a hardcore base and need only have the surface skimmed off and relaid? Is the grass path across a lawn actually hardcore underneath? A spade will soon tell you. Matters like these need to be explored early on, because they will be messy and expensive to put right. They need to be planned for properly.

Paths may be uneven but serviceable for several more years. Perfection is rarely vital.

The golden yews are healthy but way out of scale. You could retain the narrow entrance or prune them back to slender sentinels.

Buried structures

Drought can be a most useful tool in replanning a garden, for it will show up those parts of a lawn where there are old paths or hard structures underneath. Maybe a concrete pond that leaked has been broken up and left in situ with a layer of turf over the top. It would only be visible as a yellow patch of grass in very dry weather.

Foundations of old sheds and outbuildings can show up in the same way. There is no need, of course, to worry about these early on. They can be dug out in future years when more pressing matters than an even lawn have been dealt with. Lawns are easily dug and quick to heal and come last on the list of priorities when rejuvenating a garden.

But if you want to plant where there are the remains of older constructions in the soil, then you need to dig them out, or at least to know early on what size of task awaits you. Heavy concrete or brick foundations can be hard work to dig out and bulky to dispose of. There is a lot of sense in making some trial diggings, to establish how far they extend. It may be that you could break up all this concrete and use it and any other rubble, stone or brick, in the foundations of a new path or steps. It beats paying for them to be taken away in a skip, even if you have to get busy with a spade and a pick sooner rather than later.

What would this garden have without the dignity of those old trunks, even if they never bore a single apple?

Assessing the Restrictions

Garden making is never quite the entire leap of imagination we hope it will be. There are always a few dreary, practical restrictions that get in the way. I do not refer to soil and climate and landform, which are the discipline of garden making and the things that combine to make the formula of each individual garden. I mean the unproductive problems, among them four-legged pests, two-legged planning officers and facts of life like drains. We may or may not like them, but no one can ignore them.

Animal invaders

The choked undergrowth of a neglected garden is the perfect cover for animal pests, for whom over the seasons the place has assumed the nature of a sanctuary. Along comes an intruder – you, the gardener – and disrupts the way of life they have established over generations of their brief lives.

Make a realistic assessment of who is going to win the battle if you decide to try to fight them. This is largely a question of terrain. Eliminating slugs and snails from a cool, moist, stony garden might be as hopeless as keeping burrowing rabbits and leaping deer out of a garden in open country – or even, surprisingly, a garden in a suburban area, where these hungry herbivores drift about between gardens and small woodlands and railway embankments.

The burrowers

These are the animals that move in at, or below, ground level, burrowing in through hedges and under fences.

If rabbits are in a garden you soon see them, sitting on the grass in the lingering patches of sun on a summer's evening. They will have eaten to death their favourite plants long ago in a neglected garden and the evidence of present damage may not be especially obvious. But once you start to replant, the fun will begin. Rabbits are interested in anything newly planted, not just

If a view has to be heavily closed, for privacy, make the closure a focus. Bounce the view back again.

RABBIT-PROOF PLANTS

Herbaceous plants that rabbits usually leave alone once established include:

Acanthus (bear's breeches)
Aconitum (monkshood)
Agapanthus (African lily)
Ajuga (bugle)
Alchemilla (lady's mantle)
Allium (ornamental onion)
Alstroemeria

Anemone, Japanese
Aquilegia (columbine)
Colchicum
Convallaria (lily of the valley)
Cortaderia (pampas grass)
Digitalis (foxglove)
Doronicum (leopard's bane)
Erythronium (dog's-tooth violet)
Galanthus (snowdrop)
Hemerocallis (day lily)
Iris

Kniphofia (red-hot poker, torch lily)
Lupinus (lupin)
Myosotis (forget-me-not)
Narcissus (daffodil)
Paeonia (peony)
Persicaria (knotweed)
Phytolacca (pokeweed)
Polygonatum (Solomon's seal)
Pulmonaria (lungwort)
Trollius (globeflower)
Verbascum (mullein)

A good, tight, rabbit-proof fence, with the netting dug into the ground on the rabbits' side.

their favourite dishes like campanula served on a bed of succulent clove pinks with helianthemum dressing. They want to dig up new plants, to look into the hole and see exactly what it was you were trying to bury there. Gardeners really mystify them.

If yours is the kind of gardening that cannot happen with rabbits around, then you will have to deal with them. A couple of good cats make the best start. Fence them out too, with chicken wire at least 75cm (30in) tall and with another 30cm (12in) buried horizontally on the enemy's side of the fence. Wire your gates too and keep them shut. Rabbits caught inside after curfew will have to face military justice.

The sooner you start to exclude rabbits the better. Once the garden becomes unknown territory to a new generation of rabbits, keeping them out always becomes a little easier. They forget, you see. They are not terribly bright.

If you want to live with the rabbits and not exclude them, you must work with a limited palette of plants. Maybe you should still have the cats, too; rabbits breed so very fast.

Living with rabbits is not so very awful. They do get used to plants being there and their curiosity and appetite refocuses on grass and their favourite dishes once more. In the interim you will need to plant new shrubs in a ring of chicken wire fixed with bamboo canes, or to wire off whole shrubberies, until the plants are old enough to hold their own. Young sapling trees need to

Plastic spirals and tubes are an effective deterrent to many pests.

go into plastic spiral tree guards, which come in a sober dark brown as well as all those indiscreet littery pale pinks and creams. Tree tubes, for the protection of very young seedling trees, are also available in dark brown.

Badgers are protected by legislation in Britain, yet they can sometimes be terribly destructive in gardens, making their motorways through prized borders (they do not understand planning permission or private property) and uprooting sizeable shrubs time and time again, apparently for the fun of it. Once again the best tactic is to live with them, but to erect such temporary and impassable barriers as will persuade them to make their favoured routes and lavatory arrangements elsewhere.

The leapers

These are the 'airborne' pests for whom the tall barriers that keep out most human intruders offer no deterrent. Deer and squirrels are often the worst offenders.

Little muntjac deer leave a browsing line at 60–75cm (2–2 ½ ft) even on tough shrubs like rhododendron. Roe deer will nip the young shoots out of all kinds of trees and shrubs (thorny roses are their foie gras) and rub their downy antlers on young whippy saplings until the bark is shredded. Fallow are just as bad. So are red deer – but bigger.

To work reliably, deerproof fencing has to be all of 2.8m (9ft), and strong. It costs a fortune and makes the garden look like a concentration camp. If you must have it, try to hide it on a line through the middle of trees or outer shrubberies, where it is hidden to view and harder to leap because of the proximity of the plants. The outside plants must of course be sacrificial.

If the deer problem is only occasional, it is better to plant impenetrable thickets or hedges around the garden and narrow down any easy entrances and exits to something which can be given a tall gate, to be closed overnight. Deter them. Block up their usual route of entry with fencing and see if they cannot be made to adopt a new path which does not include your garden.

Grey squirrels are sadly becoming a serious plague in Britain and there is not much to be done about them, short of shooting or poisoning by professionals. The damage they can cause to young trees, tearing off the bark in long shreds until the branches are almost bare, is a distressing sight, especially if you planted the trees 15 years ago.

(Red squirrels are, of course, a protected species in Britain and do not cause such damage. They are rare because their preferred foods – Scots pine and hazel – are also rare in quantity nowadays.)

Beneficial beasts

Aside from these larger four-legged inhabitants, old gardens will have a wealth of harmless and beneficial mini-beasts living in every part of the garden, from newts and insects in ponds to moths in meadows and bats in the cracks of old, torn branches. Until you start to live in a garden, you never know what wildlife is there. The best you can do is to expect there to be more than you see and to proceed cautiously with major upheavals. If you want to remove trees or hedges, get it done early enough in the season, before the birds have begun to nest. Try not to

Squirrel damage to mature tree roots.

Osier fencing used to screen a footpath from the garden. It makes you feel secluded but very mean.

be too neurotically tidy when pruning large shrubs and trees: dead wood plays host to huge numbers of beneficial insects.

If you think you may have a special habitat of some kind, perhaps a large pond, a flower-rich meadow, or a particularly ancient, lichen-rich tree, then take advice from the local Wildlife Trust on how best to incorporate the habitat into your garden-making.

Services and supplies

Underground and sometimes overhead services will always restrict garden planning to some extent. In a modern house there may still be plans showing where water and electrical services run and where drains and soakaways are located. In old houses a bit of exploration and deduction is required. But it is worth the trouble. It makes no sense to plant trees right on top of a drain or a soakaway, as it will gradually but certainly fill with roots. Nor do you want to be digging a vegetable patch where an underground cable runs, or have the branches of trees rubbing against the telephone line.

Questions of conservation

Town and country planning regulations sometimes place a surprising number of restrictions on what local inhabitants can do – of which the newcomer to an area, keen to rejuvenate a neglected patch – may be unaware. Before you decide to replace a picket fence with a wall (or a hedge), check that you are allowed to do so. There may be local ordinances governing what you can use, particularly if you live in a Conservation or Heritage Area

with strong local character in its building styles and materials.

Regulations can affect not only inanimate built structures but also the planted elements. In some areas mown grassy verges are *de rigueur* and planting them up, fencing them in or even leaving them to grow into a 'wildflower meadow' is frowned upon. Some authorities impose height restrictions on hedges.

Trees of surprisingly small dimensions may be protected by law (see page 54). If you anticipate the need for significant tree works, find out whether any individual or blanket Tree Preservation Orders have been imposed on any of your trees by the local authority. If so, you will need to consult and get permission to proceed before work starts. Occasionally permission is not forthcoming and for good reasons pertaining to a wider landscape than your garden, but more often the authorities will respect well-intentioned gardening, especially when it involves planting new trees also. But do consult first.

Rights of way

Think about footpaths and rights of way, too. If there is one across your garden you will surely know about it. But sometimes gardeners buy a country garden close to a footpath only to be enraged by what feels like a lack of privacy or security from passers-by or hikers. You may well want to plan your garden to screen the footpath, or you may fancy the idea of a captive audience for your blaze-of-colour flower garden. Think about it. But if you want seclusion, it wants preserving from the start, while you thin trees and shrubberies, or it wants planting anew in the early stages.

Trees close to the house, especially in hot climates, have great charm. But beware of damage to the structure.

Understanding your own needs

What do you want from your garden? What jobs does it have to do? Is it to be a junior cycle-track, a sculpture gallery, an outdoor dining-room, somewhere to lose yourself and unwind with the weeding, or a place for wild poolside parties? Forget the plants for a few moments if you can, and ask yourself these questions. You may surprise yourself with the answers.

One thing is certain: gardens are never made by accident. Even the least complicated garden exists because someone has decided that this precise arrangement is exactly what they want and that this is what they are prepared to maintain. Without care and maintenance there is no gardening. So it is as well to be sure that what you create – the space and the picture you make outdoors – also fulfils all the practical purposes it must serve as well.

Scribble all your garden's functions down on a piece of paper, and then list them in order of priority. More often than not, special plants and gardening come lower down the list than making a space which is usable and practical. A design that is functional has to come first. I find that rather refreshing, and fun. It means that, in thinking how to tackle an overgrown garden, you can relax a little about the plants, and concentrate first on making the thing work and do its job. You can decorate it later.

What must your garden provide for you?

- Privacy
- Shade
- Another space to eat in
- A play area for children
- An environment suitable for pets

It is essential to know what functions the garden must perform before you begin to think about plants. Make a list of priorities before you start to enable you to perfect your plan.

Social Needs

We rejuvenating gardeners don't have the freedom of the 'blank canvas' of a new, empty garden on which to impose our plans. We come with our list of ideas of what we want from our plot in the future, but are faced with the legacy of past planting. Usually this takes the form of a mass of vegetation, some of which needs to be removed for us to realize our ambitions.

The first task is often to create some degree of space and light around the house. At the centre of an overgrown garden there is frequently an overgrown house in a tea-cosy of vegetation. It may be that building works to the house mean all that vegetation has to go, for repointing, re-roofing, new drains and so on. But if the house is sound but smothered, what then?

A curtain of creepers

A house that is entirely covered with plants looks more silly than romantic. If you want convincing, read Virginia Woolf's description, in *Orlando*, of the dampness and creepers that marked the onset of the 19th century. It will have you running for the secateurs immediately. Usually 30 percent of cover is more than enough to

The marks left on walls by ivy and self-clinging creepers can take several years to disappear.

An attractively overgrown doorway, where practical, lends great calm to a garden. No signs of all those busy people.

make a house look embraced by its garden, where such a connection is needed. A low thatched country cottage might well benefit from such intimacy, whereas an imposing Edwardian town house might be better with its architectural detail on view. A simple, clean-lined modern house may also be better uncomplicated by splurges of foliage, and dressed instead by the clean shapes of adjacent shrubs or bamboos.

If you do keep a great deal of cover on a house, be it wisteria or ivy or Virginia creeper, retain it in generous blocks and not in a thin moustache along the bottom of the walls. Try to keep some windows within the area that is covered. It will be a regular job to keep climbers cut back from them so that light is not restricted, but the cosy effect is worth the trouble. Equally with doorways, if you like a calm, romantic look, leave the occasional shrub restricting or overhanging a doorway. Clip it into shape if needs be. It speaks subliminal volumes of peacefulness.

Trees near the house

Trees close to houses are a perennial worry to home owners. Insurers would have us worry even more. Sometimes (and especially on clay soils where shrinkage and heave are more marked) a tree too close to a house will adversely affect the building. Sometimes it will not. It depends on the soil type, and the species of tree, and the climate, and the kind of foundations. There is little virtue in making any generalization about whether a tree close to a house should be removed. But of this you can be sure: absolute safety is a lousy design principle. Who wants to be holed up in a safe house?

If you feel there is cause for concern, then consult a tree surgeon. Meanwhile, think about the qualities of the tree. Is it a massive cuckoo of a lime tree, gradually overwhelming your nest, or is it a less ambitious species? Does it block a view, such as your culinary vista from the kitchen sink? Does it make your only paved seating area cold, miserable and shady, or does it give you just the deep shade you want to set out a dining table for long al fresco lunches or late dinners, with candles and paper lanterns in the branches? Is it somewhere to sit and smoke a really good cigar? Do the benefits repay you for the gloom it produces indoors in summer? An old spreading apple or mulberry or cherry by the door, even when it is past its best, can be a wonderful thing. Do not act in haste.

Spaces for children

There is no need to be ashamed of wanting a lawn. Today there are pressures to make us feel lawns are environmentally wasteful, green deserts in which no creature lives. To some extent that is true. But in a maritime, cool-temperate climate, grass is nevertheless what happens in open spaces where trees have no chance to grow. It is the vernacular surface of the

A vegetable patch is fine, but children do need space to play.

Screening by the door creates immediate privacy between adjoining back gardens.

climate, and gravels or hard landscaping look less comfortable and need more maintenance than in a hotter, drier continental climate. A lawn, so long as it is not pointlessly large, is a kind surface upon which to look and upon which to play. If a garden with an open centre of grass is considered old-fashioned, well, does it really matter? It is a practical and sociable surface where children can play games and run about, and there are any number of other ways of making the garden more modern, by the way you plant and design around the lawn. Children need such spaces. You may find, however, that they enjoy playing in and out of the complications of the garden, the trees and beds and borders, just as much as in the spaces. They need both.

If having a large open space for grass means major clearance, of trees or borders, then clear. Think of the open spaces as the relief – the foil – for the busier, flowerier parts of the garden. Better a calm open space than dreary, unloved borders you have too little time to maintain. Think of a swimming pool in the same way, if you intend to install one – as a calm, formal moment in the garden, perhaps enclosed, but still offsetting the areas of richer planting. Make sure it is aesthetically part of the garden – an outdoor room, not a damp outdoor cupboard.

Privacy

How much privacy do you want from your garden? Houses in deep country may revel in long-distance views, and only ever catch the eye of God or of a storm. In urban areas it is different. There will probably be fences which separate your garden from the next one. The houses may be close together, semi-detached or terraced, and privacy, if required, will need to be created.

How do you feel about your neighbours? Do you want eyeball-to-eyeball contact every time you both step outside your back doors, or do you want your garden to be a hidden kingdom where you need acknowledge no one? Do you want complete and solid privacy, from a fence or evergreens, at least to eye-height, or would you prefer to be ringed by a tracery of deciduous trees? It is not an easy decision. Privacy is only gained at the price of reduced sunlight and views. Sometimes the views which are reduced are your neighbour's. Sometimes a neighbour's garden can itself be the perfect backdrop for your style of gardening: you can 'borrow' next door's garden. But if the house next door changes hands and the new owner erects a cheap and nasty garage right behind the focal pergola you spent all winter constructing, what then? If you have great ambitions for your gardening, then there is virtue in making yourself absolute master of all you can survey, by appropriate planting.

Peace and quiet

A silent garden is a wonderful thing. Absolute silence is almost impossible, for gardens are full of their own special noises, of bird song and the sound of wind in the branches, foliage rustling and perhaps water playing. But there may be sounds, and even smells, you want to block out. The worst and most common source of noise is traffic. The more you thicken the planting, the more you will keep it out, baffling it until it becomes acceptably hidden. If need be, think about turning a garden round, transferring the focus and social areas to the opposite end of the site, if that will give you room to plant better insulation.

"Ice and lemon, darling? And shall I bring your book?"

Movable seats catch the moment, in or out of the sun.

Somewhere to sit

Places to sit, or rather places to stop and look and enjoy the garden in comfort, matter a great deal to some people, and not at all to others. I have known a private garden of several acres with not a seat to be found, because it was a compulsive gardener's garden, and all the available resources were spent on plants and doing. At the opposite extreme are gardens, usually institutional ones, where memorial benches line every path at fixed intervals, each visible from the next, as if to enjoy the garden is some dreadful, exhausting chore, as if the benches are there to mark accident blackspots where the donors fell during the terrible ascent to the rose garden: 'In Memoriam Albert and Edith Pryng, now in the Rose Garden forever'.

Seating in gardens is important. If you like to sit in the garden, consider the options. Do you like fixed seating in formal positions – say, looking down a pair of long borders – which forms an architectural feature of the garden, and from which

the garden is meant to be appreciated? Or do you like to pull a deck-chair into the shade of a tree with a good book and a long drink? In either case, you need to get to know your garden, and see how it is affected by sun and by wind. Where does the last of the sunlight fall for pre-dinner drinks on a summer's evening? Is it worth spending a lot of money on a terrace on the east side of the house, if it never gets the sun when you get home in an evening? Does the wind always eddy on that particular corner of the house?

Seating, whether movable or fixed, is an important part of the decoration of any garden, as well as having a major function. In a small garden, it may be the most significant and prominent piece of hardware in the garden. So give it thought. Give it some imagination. And be prepared to spend good money on getting something attractive or perhaps an original design. It will give you pleasure for ever, and you can take it with you if you move house.

Lighting

As the years go by, garden lighting is becoming more and more sophisticated and safe, and more and more used. Gardens at night have a wholly different atmosphere from the daytime. Shadows give a new dimension, and many perfumes reach their peak after dark. Why hide indoors when you can take a late stroll to breathe in the perfume of night-scented stocks (vanilla coffee), put your nose into the elephantine trumpets of *Datura metel* (clean, and sweet as soap), or bathe in honeysuckle and regale lilies (the heavenly seraglio). Consider whether you would like to be able to use your garden at night. It is simple and cheap enough to install some lighting in the garden. But plan for it at the beginning, and lay the cables underground while you are making a mess, at the start.

With care, you can do so much for a garden with lighting. Think beyond the usual halogen spot on the back of the house. That kind of light is flat and hard and high, and frequently also floodlights your neighbour's garden, which is an unforgivable thing to do. It is an invasion of privacy of the worst kind. On the

Be generous when planning how much hard paving you want. Think about what kind of surface would suit the house.

other hand, perhaps a light inside a summerhouse, with lanterns outside it, and an up-lighter or two used in shrubberies to show of the architectural foliage of a hardy palm or cordyline or *Aralia elata*? White or very pale yellow light is kindest outdoors. Pools of red, green and blue make the garden look more like the Ghost Train at a travelling fair. If you want colours to work, use them very sparingly, or very cleverly, or not at all. Get some advice.

Everything in its place

Your list of the garden's functions is likely to include a few more basic necessities. Storage might be one: for tools, bicycles, garden furniture – even accommodation for plants, in the form of a greenhouse. Keen gardeners will want compost heaps. Outdoor cooks will want barbecues. If all or any of these items are dear to your heart, try to find a place for them in some accessible part of the garden.

You may like to dry clothes outdoors. Unfortunately washing does not dry at night. Nor does it dry during the day if you put the line or rotary dryer in some secluded little space between trees, out of the wind and sun. Decide whether to have a straight line or rotary dryer, and choose a place where it can remain permanently erected without making the garden look like a scene from Paint Your Wagon. Find a place where, if it compromises some views across the garden, it does not ruin them all.

Another thing: life is short, isn't it? Is there time for those little nylon slip-over condoms which hide collapsed rotary dryers, any more than there is time for knitted spare-toilet-roll holders? On with the gardening, please!

Good benches, but oddly placed; too far apart for friendly conversation, but firmly positioned to address each other.

Do you enjoy gardening in the shade, or would you rather hide or pave the shady areas?

Gardening Needs

When it comes to practical gardening, we all have our own likes and dislikes. Sorting out an old garden can be the perfect chance to give yourself the kind of gardening you like, and perhaps to cut out the parts you do not enjoy. Try to look at the garden with fresh eyes. Do you like it as it stands? What does it lack that would please you – the gardener?

Finding your style

Ask yourself first of all what style of garden you aim to achieve. Informal gardens more easily come out of the chaos of wildly overgrown gardens. But formality can also be achieved. It may mean more clearance, but it can be done. You may be able to save and re-use elements in the garden, by planning for some of the larger plants to focus a small vista, or to use them as the backing to a seat or sculpture. Evergreens like holly, box, yew and Portugal laurel can be hard pruned and clipped into formal shapes with great success.

Contrary to most people's initial expectations, formal gardens are faster to re-establish than informal gardens. This is perhaps because in a formal garden the spaces and shapes are the primary elements. Clear the spaces and recut the shapes and you are there. Colour is easily replaced, as annual bedding-out, in beds or pots.

In informal gardens the element of time comes into play much more. We expect to see 'natural' maturing trees which do not look as if they have just been given major surgery, as well as relaxed borders full of flower colour. This takes time to create and time to heal after surgery. You cannot buy or re-establish a relaxed look in the same way that you can buy large pieces of topiary and shapely specimen trees for the formal garden.

Let there be light

Serious wild-gardeners or eco-gardeners might choose to keep their overgrown gardens full of trees and let them develop as woodland, with a little gardening in some newly opened glades. But in smaller gardens heavy, root-riddled shade is a desperate limitation on the variety of plants you can grow, as well as being rather dreary close to a house if unpaved. You can often have a good spring garden amongst the roots of trees, using spring flowers such as snowdrops, scillas, bluebells, aconites and wood anemones. And you can have moments of delicious simplicity with moss and ferns. But nine times out of ten, rejuvenating a garden for most people's purposes means clearance of overgrown trees on a considerable scale.

Let there be colour

As you readmit light to the garden, so the opportunity for colour will re-emerge. With the trees and shrubs thinned to a more comfortable distance, the root competition will be less cruel and you can begin to grow some of the larger woodland perennials in dappled shade. Shrubs will ripen flowering wood in the sunlight once more, and begin to bloom again. It may be that much of the shrub layer of the garden has been killed by shade, and you need to replant.

Think about what kinds of colour remain in the garden. Is it a spring garden, full of bulbs and shrubs for early colour? Will it go to sleep after early summer and be resolutely green until next spring? Did it rely on bedding out to provide all the mid- to late-season colour? If so, do you enjoy bedding out, or would you rather move to permanent planting?

Look to see if there is any remaining herbaceous planting in the garden. Sometimes herbaceous perennials will survive decades of neglect, waiting there patiently for someone to come along, free them of suffocating weeds, feed them and persuade them to pop their corks once more. The members of the lily family are great survivors. So are peonies, golden rod and Japanese anemones.

Consider whether you want herbaceous colour for late summer and autumn? Think about how you wish to dispose the colour around the garden. If you want to have a traditional and prominent high-summer showpiece, of roses, campanulas and delphiniums, then it may be easier to plan for late colour to be focused elsewhere. Do not feel you have to make everywhere colourful all the time. Remember winter colour, too. Is there room for winter jasmine, witch hazels, or even one majestic *Rhododendron arboreum*?

Let there be perfume

Imagine a garden with no perfume. I bought one once. I knew it had all too few plants in it, and I was prepared to develop it. But the course of that first year was misery. It was like giving up smoking. Every time I met sarcococca or philadelphus or regale lilies in someone else's garden, I felt a 'twinge of desire to have them at home. Not a train-spotter's desire to tick it off, but a desire to be able to enjoy it at leisure, in comfort and at home.

For perfume is an important (if inessential) quality of gardens. You can manage without it, but why on earth should you? So pack in plenty of perfume. Plan for it. Curious that, although we talk freely enough about colour clashes, no one ever speaks of perfumes clashing. It seems one cannot have too much or too many perfumes, and therefore be as profligate as your sense of design will allow.

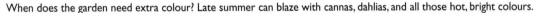

When does the garden need extra colour? Late summer can blaze with cannas, dahlias, and all those hot, bright colours.

Let there be variety

Keen gardeners and plantsmen are a hungry lot. The desire to grow and to get to know new plants is never far away, however satisfying the garden may be as it stands. But if the garden at present strikes you as plain boring, then you will need to make space for new plants, in beds or perhaps in rough grass. Maybe there is a collection of favourite plants to be urgently housed or developed – a harem of high-class hellebores, perhaps, or hoi polloi hardy geraniums? If they have specialized tastes, then plan to have sufficient space which is suitably cool and shady, or boggy, or gravelly and hot. Think about whether your collection is going to be happiest spread through the garden as a recurring motif, of whether you want to grow it as a formal collection in its own hallowed plot, where you can easily compare shape with shape and colour with colour. Having a recurring theme in a garden can be a useful way of giving the garden unity. But it can also lead you to commit the deadly sin of making all parts of the garden feel the same. Take care that the garden is designed by you and not your beloved collection.

Let there be shelter

Wind is a ruthless partner and a relentless redesigner of gardens. Unless you can create some shelter, such gardening as you achieve will always be courtesy of the prevailing winds. Watch your garden over the first year, and talk to the local people. See where the strongest winds come from, and the coldest ones. This will tell you where and when you need shelter.

There is many a fine garden made in exposed places and climates where winter lasts seven months out of twelve. Here the need to keep out cold drying winter winds is a major factor in designing the garden. It may drive you to make all your summer views internal ones, looking across the garden rather than beyond it. When the leaves fall in autumn, you will then have the bigger part of the year to appreciate the views through a tracery of trunks and branches. But in summer you will at least have some shelter, in which to grow less iron-clad species, and in which to relax and enjoy the summer's gardening. Be wary of planting wholly coniferous shelter belts, or you will lose all your views all the time. It is a desperate measure for desperate circumstances only.

Shelter and long views do not often coincide. Here an outbreak of suburban Leyland cypresses is set to hide the distant quarry.

Even fairly slight boundary trees can give a good sense of enclosure in summer.

In warmer climates, the summer winds may be the ones to cause trouble, ragging soft new foliage and withering young shoots at their most tender stage. At the seaside, the problem may be salt-laden winds, which will burn the foliage of many species, for a mile or more inland.

Perhaps your garden already has more than enough shelter. Perhaps it is choked with trees, but still in an exposed location. This is the time to be especially careful when thinning to let in light. It must be done gradually, over a few years, letting the trees that are retained get used to bearing the full brunt of the wind without help from neighbours. Try to establish a mixed age range in your shelter planting, so that there are always young trees coming along as others give up the struggle. Never let the moment come when all the shelter trees mature and die together. Be prepared also for shelter trees not to be fine, balanced specimens, but to be things shaped by the wind, sacrificial lambs to the slaughter of the wind, for the sake of protecting more important plants further inside the garden.

Taking out trees sometimes lets wind in from new directions. A tree that has perhaps stood in the face of year-long westerlies for 40 years may, if suddenly exposed to unaccustomed north-easterlies, blow over with the first gale. Exposed gardens call for careful, gradual management of the wind.

Even in towns wind can be a problem. Tall buildings especially can create vicious eddies in gusty weather. Plants grown at the foot of a tall wall will often lean forward, not because they are drawn to the light, but because they are pushed forward by wind perpetually bouncing off the wall surface.

The golden rules with shelter planting are: 1) remove it very carefully, if you must, and 2) plant it, if you need it, as soon as you possibly can.

Water features

Dealing with water is never easy. Old ponds frequently need major clearance of silt and debris, and afterwards leak. If you want a new pond in a garden, think about it early on, as water is not one of those things you can put anywhere. A 'natural' pond always looks most comfortable at a low point in the garden. Falling water looks best running down a natural slope and not from some artificial mound. Make some exploration of old ponds in good time, so you have an idea of how much silt there will be to dispose of, and how its disposal could practically be managed. Where will all the silt go? Could it be reused for building up levels elsewhere? Is the water supply to the pond in good order and reliable? What is the depth of water? Will that depth support those plants I wish to grow?

Formal gardens, both level and terraced, allow for a more imaginative approach to water, up to a point where water becomes a medium of liquid sculpture, static or fluid, with which one can play tricks. So water may form part of your design structure, and may involve considerable hard-landscaping costs.

'Natural' ponds always make most sense and look happiest at a low point in the garden.

The old shed – do you need it at all? Do you cover it up in creepers? Whitewash it? Demolish it and erect another one elsewhere?

Buildings

Garden sheds are rarely found where you want them. If there is one – and everyone needs storage for tools and machines – then consider whether it should be moved to a more discreet position, or if it could be made a virtue where it stands? Would a dose of whitewash and *Clematis montana* give it an ornamental as well as a practical function?

Some gardeners feel deprived without a greenhouse. Nothing can quite replace the pleasure of growing your own plants from seed and making your own cuttings. If a greenhouse is going to be needed now or later, plan where it must go while you plan the rest of the garden. Will it be hidden and away from the main ornamental areas? Will it have short and easy, paved access from the house, and will it have heat and light and power?

For most purposes, a greenhouse that receives less than full light is preferable. Blasting all-day sun means that much more attention to watering and ventilation will be required in summer. If all you need is a propagating house, to raise cuttings and plants

from seed, then an open east- or even north-facing position may be far easier to manage. It will not have the benefit of as much of the sun's warmth, but temperatures will be more stable. It will mean you can place it in a more out-of-the-way position, and save the better sunny spaces for gardening. It will survive a few days in summer without watering if you go away.

A hot spot might be the place for a summerhouse or gazebo. Garden buildings serve both as architectural ornament and also as somewhere to sit when the weather is not quite warm enough to be outside unprotected. They extend the social season of the garden. If you are anxious to have as much time as possible in your garden, consider having an enclosed summerhouse.

Fruit and vegetables

If you want to grow fruit and vegetables, you will need to relinquish some good gardening ground for the purpose. It needs to be light and open above all else. Poor soil can be improved with time and effort. Be realistic about the kinds of things you wish to grow. Of course fresh home-grown vegetables taste better than bought ones, but do you have the time to manage a large vegetable patch? Would you be better off and happier just growing salads, carrots, beans and tomatoes – things which taste so much better fresh – or would you enjoy going the whole hog with brassicas, main-crop potatoes and the works? Do you see vegetable gardening as all hard work and pest control, and definitely for the under-forties, or will you just love it for ever? Be honest with yourself. Would a couple of small apple trees relieve you of the urge to produce, or do you crave an orchard?

If you are lucky enough to have an old orchard, then you have the choice of getting it back in productive order, by pruning, or of letting it coast into old age unpruned, producing what fruit it will, and perhaps forming a pretty structure under which to practise a grid pattern of meadow gardening, set out between close-mown paths.

Easy access

The credo of labour-saving for its own sake can lead to some dreadfully boring gardening. Nevertheless, when planning a garden it is satisfying to make things practically efficient for yourself.

Turn tricky slopes into steps or terraces if it makes you happier about the use and look of the garden, but make sure

Raised beds or troughs can offer the physical pleasures of gardening, but from a chair.

Sloping grass paths are informal and easy going for barrows. But you might prefer to build steps and a terrace wall.

you can still get barrows or mowers from one level to another with sufficient ease. Arrange it so that compost bins can be as near as possible to their source of vegetable matter, as well as being suitably hidden. Put a tap at the bottom of the garden if you see the need.

Make sure you can get from A to B – kitchen to bins, back door to summerhouse, or round the winter circuit of perfumed shrubs – with dry feet.

Think about the hard surfaces generally. Would you prefer to see paved rather than gravel surfaces for ease of maintenance, or is the softer appearance of gravel vital to the garden? Is there too much paving all together? It can happen, especially in the wake of a determined labour-saver.

Is there quite simply too much close mowing for you to cope with every week? Would it be better to allow some of it to go to rough grass with bulbs in it, or to meadow gardening? Would you cope with cutting rough grass less frequently, and have you space to store a heavier-duty mower for the purpose? Could you learn to use and sharpen a scythe instead?

Simplification

If you take on a large garden and have neither the time nor the experience to cope with it, think about how it might be simplified. Reduce the amount of labour-intensive, decorative gardening, especially around the edges of the garden. This will allow you to concentrate on getting the structure in order. Perhaps some flowery, labour-intensive beds nearer the house would be most appropriate.

Grass down that wonderful sweep of orchard lavender; it's inspired planting but hard to keep weed-free (top).

Do away with little beds around trees which have to be weeded. Lawn alone, or even rough grass, would be quite appropriate here (bottom).

Lawn running imperceptibly into a border of roses and feverfew looks very romantic, but how do you stop the grass infiltrating the plants? Wouldn't it be easier to cut back the turf a little, and make space at the front of the bed to run a hoe in? Remember that wild gardens are always notoriously difficult to keep looking good right through the season (top).

Focus on the most hard-working plantings of annuals and perennials around the house. Artful drifts of colour in the wilder parts of the garden can simply be grassed down, until you have time to cope (bottom).

When Ethel Merman used to belt out the song 'I'm still Here' in Follies, she was not thinking of rhododendrons. But, like her, hardy rhododendrons will survive practically anything. In old age, low branches will root down and start new plants so that, even if the centre dies out, the satellites will continue.

To reduce the size or restore stability, old trunks can be cut hard back in winter to regrow. Grafted specimens will produce a forest of dreary *Rhododendron ponticum* suckers, but those on their own roots will produce shoots of the intended named cultivar.

It is kinder to the plant to cut half at a time, allowing one side of the plant to shoot out and recover before cutting back the rest.

PART II Doing the Job

 Waiting or starting

 Eradicating weeds

 Plan of attack

 Clearing old hard landscape

 Financing the work

 Pruning trees and shrubs

 Permissions and possibilities

 New structure planting

 Seasonal jobs

 New hard landscaping

 First aid for gardeners

 General replanting

 Timing

 Lawns and fine path surfaces

 Clearance

Waiting or Starting: the Pros and Cons

There you are in the new house. You have been here a week, and it's a shining summer morning. You stand and look at this crazy overgrown garden, itching to get stuck in. You may not be sure where to start, but that is not going to stop you: there's a garden to be made.

Now I hate saying this, I really do: but could you just hang on a moment? Can I persuade you to take stock and pause before you do anything irreversible? Some people say you should wait a year – a year, can you believe it? – before you start a new garden. I say

you can't wait, and all that enthusiasm must not be squashed. So let's just look at the pros and cons of starting at once.

In favour of starting immediately

There may be pressing factors that make you want to start as soon as possible. You may have a garden shed full of treasured plants, potted up from your last garden, and urgently in need of planting out. The lawn may be waist-high and the beds full of plants and serious weeds. Your best bet here might be to scythe

Knowing what is below as well as above the soil is vital to help you proceed. For instance, if you moved into this garden in autumn you might never know such displays of small bulbs were here until they surprised you in the spring.

Does an overgrown lawn daunt you? Strim it, mow it, and it will soon be in hand. The real problem is the golden leyland cypress which will soon smother the blue spruce. Which would you keep?

or strim down the lawn, mow it short, and take off some turf and dig out of it a holding bed somewhere – somewhere you can plant your treasures temporarily. Who knows what running weeds are in the borders, waiting to infest your new plants?

You may want to chop back some rampant clematis or forsythia which is blocking the path to the back door. Well, that's fine. Do it, because if you want them to regrow later, these particular plants will be obliging enough (but check whether all plants in your way will be equally able to recover).

It may be that the house is in worse condition than the garden, and you want to start outdoors because you cannot afford to work on the house yet. It may be you have a firm and fixed idea of what you want to do in the new garden – make a jungle of exotic foliage, or a heather garden, or a wild garden of naturalized perennials. But whatever the case, it does pay to wait for a season – a year if you can bear it – to see what are the real advantages and disadvantages of the site. Until you have lived there you can never be sure.

Discovering the garden's secrets

Curiously, the better the condition of a garden, the more reason there is for waiting, because you never know what plants are going to appear. Especially if you move in during the winter. You may find in spring that every square inch is filled with bulbs – and more may appear in autumn. There may be bulbs under the trees. There may be peonies in the rough grass. There may be bluebells just where you wanted to make a heather garden – and who ever heard of anyone managing to clear an area completely of bluebells? They would be a nuisance weed for ever.

The repair of crumbling walls, however charming, needs to be done before the wall collapses and the structure and materials are lost entirely. If it has to be done, do it soon, because it will be messy and expensive. New plantings below can then mature in safety.

Don't take out trees until you are sure they have to go. They may appear gaunt but perhaps they provide much-needed privacy in summer.

The advantages of waiting

Waiting will tell you whether the existing planting is healthy, and if that cherry tree is just slow to leaf or actually dead, and whether the roses are riddled with rust and mildew. It will tell you whether the garden has been planted with the kind of lack of colour co-ordination that will exasperate you for the rest of your life. Better surely to sort that out at the beginning than to bolt all your planting on to it.

Waiting will tell you if the soil is fertile with plenty of worms in it, or gutless and worked-out. It will tell you if the garden is a frost pocket or prone to drought where there are tree roots. It will tell you where the sun falls in winter and summer, and therefore where not to put a terrace or a summerhouse.

It will tell you whether it's a haven for rabbits, slugs and snails and whether you would rather not grow hostas if they are going to be riddled with holes without constant slug pelleting.

Be content that the garden is not slug and snail heaven before you decide to put in major plantings of hostas or ligularias. Better to plant to suit the local conditions than be forever fighting a losing battle against endemic pests.

A good foundation

None of this means you cannot make progress in the first year. You can see to the basic housekeeping, by mending the fences and making them pet-proof, by getting the lawn in hand so the children can play, and by starting to deal with obvious weeds like brambles and bindweed. By simply maintaining the garden and living in it you will get to know its problems and possibilities.

Waiting, in a word, will tell you what your true options are. And all the time you can be matching your aspirations against the physical realities of the garden, and deciding what will or won't work. Sometimes the first idea holds good. Sometimes you will come up with something 10 times more exciting.

Time to plan

All through that first season your plans will be maturing, and you can be thinking how best to approach the work itself. Spend time in the garden simply looking. Play with different ideas in your imagination. Nothing you ever do in a garden is irrevocable. You can change your mind as often as you like. The best plans are often those which have developed and refined themselves along the way, as one part of the garden develops and the living reality suggests a useful alteration to the next part. But the more you can plan in advance the better. It is all time gained, and less effort to be undone.

Planning a garden need not be daunting. You do not need to be a draughtsman or produce masterplans on paper. The important thing is to consider what you are doing and what you want to achieve. Think not only about the bit of the garden you are rejuvenating, but about how it affects the whole design. Remind yourself not to work in a piecemeal way, and you will be well on the way to success.

Some animals will nibble herbaceous plants such as these hostas, and eat the shoots of young trees and roses. See what mammals use the garden over 12 months, and decide which can co-exist with your style of gardening, and which will have to be excluded.

Developing an empty garden is so much easier than a congested one, although there are no plants around which to develop the garden. Spraying with glyphosate will clean up grass and perennial weeds before you start to dig, but don't assume that one application will do the job entirely. They'll be back.

The owner of this new house is indoors, weeping on a packing case. If you or a builder are going to lay turf, it should either go down in autumn or spring. If it has to go down in summer it must be regularly watered. On a totally blank canvas, turf can be the easiest, most convenient way to start a garden. Everything else can follow. So cheer up.

Plan of Attack

As you think about what you want from the garden, a plan of what to do will form in your mind. There will be a list of jobs and mini-projects needed to complete the work. This section of the book will help you sort out how to prioritize those jobs involved in rejuvenating a garden. But before you start to plan the work, ask yourself some basic questions about the timing of the work, and your short-term and long-term wishes for the garden.

Would you like to have the areas round the house clean and colourful in six months' time? That is not an unreasonable idea. It makes family life so much easier and enjoyable. No one wants to live in a building site for any longer than necessary, and if you start working on too many parts of the garden at once it can make the whole place unusable. There is great sense in getting somewhere near the house into a reasonable condition first.

What do you see as the long-term future of the garden? If the trees are all on their last legs, then there is going to have to be a programme of felling and replacement. If they are not to be dealt with in one fell swoop at the start, then how do you see it happening? Half now, and half in another five years? Critical ones near the house and open spaces felled now, and one every year after that? Could they all wait for 10 years, and perhaps ultimately be someone else's responsibility? Think about it, and decide what would suit you. It's your garden, and there is no absolute right and wrong. The only limiting factors are how often you want the upheaval of tree felling or dismantling.

Know what you like

Be realistic about how much energy you want to put into the garden now and in 10 years' time.

The ideal for you might be to make a clean, modern garden that will survive on the minimum of care now and in the future, so you can enjoy the space and take all the foreign holidays you want without worrying about the planting getting out of control.

You may feel you want a really hard-working garden full of colour and unusual plants. Great! Have one. But if it breaks your heart to see your garden get out of hand, try not to mix the

What comes first for you? Would you open up the view immediately, or would you wait and see what winds the trees keep out first?

a mess, there is great satisfaction in laying down bones for the future of the garden, even if you know you will never see them mature. (Many of us like to garden that way wherever we live, just for the satisfaction of knowing the garden will mature into something greater than the sum of its present parts.) So ask yourself whether the garden needs some investment for the very long term – a new line of trees from the road, or an orchard for your grandchildren to play in?

A realistic time-scale

When might you like to have completed the work on the garden? Gardens, I know, are never really finished; there is always something to be done, some new development twinkling in the eye. But how soon would you like to get the garden sorted out and the major rejuvenation completed?

Giving some thought to this can be most encouraging. Instead of the project being a huge task stretching endlessly into the next five years, you can offer yourself some light at the end of the tunnel. Give yourself a date. Say that in perhaps three years I want to have rebuilt the terrace and put some big flower beds under it, taken out four sizeable trees, planted shrubs for shelter and privacy, and laid out a vegetable garden.

You can then allocate the various jobs to the three seasons. Most people's practical priorities in such a list would be to start with the tree felling, then move on to shelter planting, rebuilding works and the preparation of beds, and finally the planting of shrubs and flowers. But your short-term and long-term priorities may alter that.

shrub and herbaceous planting too much, so that if needs be you can easily simplify the garden later by grassing down a few herbaceous areas. So often keen gardeners in old age break their hearts over trees and shrubs they have planted and which are now maturing, but which have filled up with weeds at ground level because they were unable to keep up with the maintenance of herbaceous plants underneath.

Some gardeners are happy with a romantic muddle and will not worry about a garden that has got distinctly woolly around the edges. But if you are a worrier, consider keeping the garden simplifiable, for your own satisfaction.

One of the great pleasures of gardening is to be able to plan for the very long-term future. When someone inherits a house and garden which has been in the family for years and is now in

With a big overgrown garden to tackle, it sometimes pays to divide it up. Give yourself some quick screening and make an area you can use and enjoy soon. A *Clematis montana* and a few pots, and you have a pleasant screen, hiding all the ongoing work at the back of the garden.

When you plan paths and paving, make sure you allow space for your style of planting. Plants spilling over onto paving can considerably reduce an area once things start to grow. Allow for enough paving for both you and the plants and maybe a table and chairs.

Major hard landscaping is expensive and messy (left). It needs good access. Sometimes in a town garden the only access is through the house. If you want to rejuvenate as radically as this, you must do the hard landscaping first. Once you start planting, you will not want to go back to this sort of mess again.

Choose hard landscaping materials which are appropriate to the house and the locality (above). Use the fewest possible kinds of material to do the job satisfactorily. And choose the best quality you can afford. You will never regret it.

Financing the Work

Good gardening can be fabulously expensive and extraordinarily cheap. It all depends on your approach. If you have plenty of time and energy, then it is amazing what can be achieved with very little money. If you are in a hurry, and need to buy in other people's labour and large plants, then costs will spiral upwards just as far as you let them.

In most gardens, the biggest costs are the construction of hard landscaping – paths, steps, water features, fences and walls – and tree surgery. Next to these expenses, the price of planting or replanting can be slim.

Hard landscaping

Think about this as you plan the work. As a general rule it is much better to install good-quality hard landscaping and wait a little longer for the plants to mature, than it is to do a quick, cheap job on the hard landscaping for the sake of affording bigger plants. When steps begin to crumble and paving to sink, you will only regret it. So spend as much as you dare on the hard landscaping, and not least on the quality of the materials. This will be the skeleton of the garden on which the planting will hang. The better its quality, the better will be the finished picture.

Choosing materials

Think about what materials to use in the garden. Let the construction of the house itself suggest what might usefully be its complement. An old house in a traditional architectural style is best served by something which arises from that tradition. In an area where the houses are all stone, stone would be the natural choice. In a traditionally brick area, brick or stone would look right. Modern houses, freed from the age-old vernacular traditions, may readily accept a wider range of suitable surfaces, from the traditional to the modern. Old houses can, of course, accept modern materials, and it may be your choice deliberately to mix the old and the new. Most importantly, it is the scale and quality of materials used that will determine whether they work in any garden.

But the materials you choose will have a huge significance for your construction costs. Paved surfaces in natural stone or brick will cost many times as much as gravel or concrete paving. At some stage you must decide whether you can live with cheaper, synthetic materials or whether you want to pay for natural materials.

When your ideas for the garden are starting to take shape, talk to a local builder about your hard landscaping needs, and ask for an estimate for the work. It is worth asking at least one more builder to offer you a price too, making sure you present to him exactly the same scope of work and quality of materials.

Planting costs

Put together an estimated list of planting needed to rejuvenate the garden, and rough out some costs based on garden-centre prices. Keep it simple: perhaps in a medium-sized garden the total might reach 12 standard trees, 40 shrubs and 70 herbaceous plants. Make extra allowance if you want to use mature containerized stock of certain key trees and shrubs, to get the garden off to a strong start. Ask for some quotations from specialist suppliers. This planting estimate and the construction estimates will give you an idea of your costs for the garden.

Phasing the work

You can now adjust your budget, by perhaps buying smaller plants, or by doing all or part of the hard landscaping yourself. But most significantly, you can adjust the costs by phasing the work over a few years.

Rejuvenating your garden over a long period for financial reasons is certainly not a problem. It is frequently much the best thing for the garden to be brought up to the mark gradually. Remember, it is you who are in a hurry, not the garden.

Taking it slowly allows you to develop the details of your design as you progress. Perhaps you might decide you would rather spend your money at this stage on a beautiful, craftsman-made iron gate between the two halves of the garden than on a new boundary fence. Perhaps a tree you carefully extricated

from smothering saplings, and around which you have based your design, suddenly blows over, unable to cope with life in the open again. Perhaps your neighbour fells some trees that were sheltering your garden. There are many, many things that affect the life of a garden, and it is as well never to assume that the only ones that will change are the ones you actively change yourself. It can be better, for the garden and the plants and for you, to tackle the rejuvenation steadily over a few years, doing what you can with your own energy as time permits. In 10 years' time you will look back with infinitely more satisfaction. Rejuvenating a garden, just like maintaining a garden, gives greatest pleasure to those who are doing it. So unless you are anxious to have the garden completed very soon for social use, why not consider taking it all very gradually and doing all you possibly can by yourself? Pay just for the things you cannot or do not wish to tackle, such as brickwork, perhaps, or high tree pruning. Buy plants in ones and twos, and propagate from them straight away. Join the local gardening societies and look in at charity markets to find a plant bargain in a yoghurt pot.

In the finished garden, notice how the saved tree at the end of the path now looks significant and established, and worth saving even in such a radical redesign. Two sociable-looking chairs suggest the hidden space around the corner.

Would you spare that tree? True, it's close to the house but it does a good job shading the terrace in a Mediterranean sea-side climate. How long would it take to get anything else nearly so grand by the sea?

Permissions and Possibilities

As your plans for tackling the garden take shape, there may be people you wish to inform about your intentions, and possibly authorities whose permissions you need to seek before work is allowed to go ahead. Think about what is involved in plenty of time. Making sure you have not only the physical means to carry out the work – contractors, hired machinery, skips, new plants – but also any legal clearances will affect the way you set about drawing up your detailed timetable of works.

Good neighbours

Not least of the people to forewarn are neighbours. On hearing the howl of a chainsaw many people – in towns especially – have the habit of thinking that the end of the world is nigh, and that you are recklessly about to cut down every tree in sight. Curtains twitch. People come outside to watch and stare. So do let the locals know what you are going to do. Make sure they know you are acting thoughtfully and for the long-term good of the garden. Don't spend a day running a chainsaw without giving them warning, or smoke out their barbecue or their washing with a bonfire.

It may be in that talking to your neighbour you discover that one of your trees or shrubs fulfils some important function in their garden, hiding a lamp standard or keeping the midday sun off the greenhouse. Why not adjust your plans to help a neighbour, if you can do so without compromising your intentions?

Co-operative neighbours are worth their weight in gold. Perhaps they will allow you convenient access through their property to barrow out a demolished wall, or to drive a mini-digger into your back garden. You may need to go on to their land to repair fences, or dismantle the overhanging branches of a tree that is to be lopped or felled. Making enemies of neighbours, for want of a little courtesy, is a disastrous thing to do. Making friends can mean you always have a helping hand to call upon.

Spare that tree

There may be formal permissions required before any work can go ahead. Towns and cities in Britain, and even country villages, frequently have Tree Preservation Orders (TPOs) placed upon certain trees, and any work to these trees must be cleared with the local authority before it can go ahead. It makes no difference whether the tree is on your land or public land:

permission must be sought. In some cases permission may not be forthcoming, and you will need to adjust your plans for the garden accordingly. It is not that local planning authorities wish to be obstructive, but rather that mature trees, on whoever's land they may be, have a value to the whole community just as much as to the garden they stand in. A little give and take is required. Often permission is forthcoming, especially if it is clear that you intend to plant more trees as part of your rejuvenation process.

It is worth sounding out the local authorities at an early stage if you envisage felling or even lopping operations on your trees. The wheels of planning departments can turn slowly, so some delay may need to be fed into your timescale. Talking to a local arboricultural officer is never a bad idea; he could be a mine of useful information and advice.

Protected zones

Usually TPOs are applied to individual trees, but sometimes a Blanket TPO is applied to preserve all the trees in a particular locality. In other protected zones, known as Conservation Areas, there is a duty to give six weeks' notice to the local planning authorities of any works to trees within the area. It may come as a surprise that what counts as a 'tree' in a Conservation Area may be little over the thickness of a wrist in diameter at what they call 'breast height', and can therefore include many a young, self-sown sycamore or ash, or even a laurel or elder that has put itself in an inappropriate place. If the work is to be carried out on a tree 'to improve the growth of other trees', then you are free do so without consultation if the tree is under 100mm (4in) in diameter at 1.5m (5ft) from ground level. These are really quite small trees, and it pays to consult first and chop later, or you can soon be in trouble with the law.

Booking ahead

Other things to check include whether the contractors whom you chose to give you an estimate for hard-landscaping work can in fact do the work when you want it done. If you intend to plant around new or repaired hard landscaping in spring and the contractor does not complete the work until summer, then you will have missed a planting season and lost valuable time. You may also have plants heeled in and taking up space intended for other purposes. The sooner they are properly planted the better.

Check that you have all the access you need for machinery or waste disposal skips. Is there room for a skip to be left in your driveway, or will it need to be in the road? If so, are permissions required? Any work that will obstruct rights of way for a period also needs to be cleared with local authorities in good time.

Find out if particular plants you want will be available at the right time. Will the nursery be able to supply you with what you want, and will it be the appropriate season for getting them in the ground? The ones to watch out for are plants required in large numbers (perhaps 100 white colchicums, or 200 plants of a special variety of box hedging), plants to be installed as extra-large specimens for instant effect, and plants of especially popular varieties. Old roses in particular are often difficult to obtain at short notice.

One of the best ways to kill a tree is to build up soil around the base of the trunk, as shown here. A skilled tree surgeon can dismantle even a large cedar with minimum damage to other plants.

Seasonal Jobs

To make the most of the time available, it is worth looking at the work to be done and seeing which jobs would be better done in summer and which in winter. Some may be just as easily done in either season. But if you plan roughly which to do when, you should never get to the frustrating stage of waiting idly by until the season changes. Some kinds of work will continue throughout the rejuvenation process, and will provide a constant occupation.

Earth moving

Earth moving is the the heaviest and messiest job in a garden. If a pond or drains are to be dug, or terracing constructed, or sloping land levelled, then this is always easiest done in summer.

The reasons are many. Clay soils compact easily, and especially when wet, so it is important to keep off the land when it is soaked in winter rain. Using heavy machinery such as a mini-digger on wet clay will produce problems for years to come. Even barrowing is harder when the soil is wet. If you need to shift 10 barrowloads of topsoil around the garden, would you rather move it dry or wet?

On light soils it is quite possible to undertake earth-moving work in winter, and so planning can be more flexible. Remember, however, that if the newly laid soil is to be seeded

In built-up areas bonfires may be rather antisocial, especially frequent ones, but they have been the mainstay of clearance in every major project in the history of gardens.

Perennial weeds like ground elder (*Aegopodium*) should never be given any quarter. When they creep back from under next-door's fence, dig them or spray them whenever there is anything visible.

with grass or turfed, that will only be possible at the end of the dry period, and you will have to live with the bare soil meanwhile. Once it is put to grass, you will of course have to keep heavy machinery – and even feet – off it until it is established.

Soil preparation

Once you know that there are no plants waiting to surprise you under the soil, areas for replanting can be dug over whenever it suits you.

If you are making new beds in turf or replanting old ones, then it is worth digging them over a few months in advance and getting some old compost or well-rotted manure into the soil to wake it up. Some humus and fibre is what is needed, rather than high amounts of nitrogen. But once the soil is bare you will have to think about weed control, for annual and perennial weed seeds will sprout immediately on moist warm soil, making your life difficult when you plant.

Clay soils again are the least accommodating as regards timing. If you dig over a heavy loam or clay soil in summer, it will dry into lumps and be difficult to cultivate unless you break it down finely at the time. Once the wet weather comes again fine cultivation will be easier. But then that is the time to start keeping off it again! Think at this stage about how you intend to improve the clay – either with composts or grit – and dig them in deeply and plentifully before you need to plant.

Tree surgery and major pruning

The removal of trees can be done at any time, but deciduous trees are more easily removed in winter. In summer the leaves make disposal a bulkier problem, and early in the year there is the likelihood of nesting birds in the branches. If you are in a position to dispose of the wood on a bonfire, then winter is better again as there are fewer plants and trees in leaf which might be scorched, and fewer neighbours out in their gardens. Better to let the leaves fall first and then compost them if you can: burning leaves is such a waste of resources. Coniferous trees can have their foliage put through a shredder to make a stack of mulch for future use. The same can be done to reduce the twigs of deciduous trees to chips.

Major pruning is best done in winter. The times to avoid are spells of extreme cold and freezing temperatures, and spells of sudden warmth which can cause trees in which the sap rises early (e.g. walnut, maple, birch) to bleed copiously from wounds. It is kinder to evergreens to cut them in late winter, so that they do not spend the entire winter leafless and unable to make energy from their leaves. Flowering cherries and plums are best pruned in late summer to avoid silver-leaf disease.

Weed control

Weeds are always best dealt with when the foliage is present and you can clearly see them to spray. Make the most of the growing season to make applications of safe chemicals (see pages 69–70), and then in winter revert to digging and uprooting.

A dead tree can be dug out any time, the sooner the better. Do not saw it off at ground level, unless you have to. Leave plenty of weight above to allow you to push the stump over, once all roots are cut.

Construction of walls and paving is normally a job for dry winter weather, when the garden is being used less and there is less general garden maintenance demanding your attention. But it is easier and more pleasant to do it in summer if you can.

Planting

Large plantings of containerized stock in summer make for a heavy burden of watering during the first season. Autumn-planted stock, whether bare-rooted or containerized, should survive the next season with no watering except in time of drought, because it has had all winter to establish its roots in the new position. It is fun and sometimes necessary to buy containerized specimens of things you really want as and when you see them, which may mean at any time of year, even in summer. But it is better to concentrate major new plantings in spring and autumn. Try to plant woody plants in autumn, and herbaceous plants, grasses and anything doubtfully hardy in spring. You may as well let the nursery take the risk of losses to winter cold, rather than you.

Construction work

Construction work is more pleasant and easier in summer, but it will wait until winter if need be. In winter when seasonal maintenance is minimal, it is good to be able to concentrate without interruption on a satisfying construction project. But remember that spells of snow cover or freezing weather may hold up the work considerably. Mortar does not set properly below freezing point.

Wisteria looks wonderful hoisting itself up into a cypress, but its shading will cause patches of the tree's foliage to turn brown and die out.

First Aid for Gardens

Never believe all that cant about old gardens being 'romantic' and 'timeless'. Time is what has made them, and time is what is running out on them. Life in an untended garden is not so much a gradual slippery slope to disorder as a battle between plants. And of course there are casualties. Winner takes all, and in the end it is usually a sycamore.

One of the first jobs as you start work on your garden, or earlier if you see the need, is to give immediate first aid to any things you may want to keep that seem to be visibly failing.

Clearance to combat shade problems

Shade is one of the biggest enemies in old gardens. Vigorous plants, whether self-sown or deliberately planted, can completely overwhelm their more modest neighbours when no gardener intervenes. Even if a plant is not smothered, it can be drawn upwards by indirect shade until it becomes etiolated, leggy and unstable.

Shade is a particular problem for evergreens which, where overlaid with other plants, lose their leaves in that part. If you know there is a sound evergreen (such as a specimen holly, or cypress, or fir) which is fast being smothered in wild clematis or

elder, then it is worth cutting out the invader as soon as possible. The sooner light is readmitted, the sooner the plant will begin to thicken its canopy again, provided the branch is not dead already. You are buying time for the plant and for your plan.

To cut or not to cut?

Sometimes the decision is not easy. If elder is spoiling a holly, then it is clear that the elder should be removed. But what if the invading plant is a mauve wisteria which has threaded its way 6m (20ft) up into the holly, or a pink *Clematis montana* 'Rubens', or both? The combination does look wonderful. But it is a slippery slope for the host tree to be so overwhelmed. Better to relieve it partially at least, so that you then have the option, in your planning, of keeping the host as a good, long-term tree.

Sometimes you may find a tree or large shrub has heaved over sideways under the weight of other plants or its own top-heaviness. Laburnum, for instance, is prone to lurch over in middle age, dragging up out of the earth its fat yellow roots. If you think you want to keep it, then prop up its trunk with a well-padded support before it breaks its roots. Bushier plants like Portugal laurel or hybrid rhododendrons may need the branches shortening back by a third, to reduce the weight and heave.

Erecting shelter

As you thin the overgrowth in a garden, lank specimens may suffer from wind and weather finding a way into the garden once more. They have to readjust to supporting themselves again without shoulder-to-shoulder help from neighbours. Some may have no trouble, while others will rock alarmingly; and unless they are species you can (and want) to prune down lower, then time or a little judicious thinning is the only cure. But watch what is happening closely, and learn from it. Erect some temporary shelter if necessary – a mechanical windbreak of plastic webbing, perhaps, or some woven hurdles – and plant tough new shelter species in the critical places for the long term.

Gently knock heavy snowfall off plants susceptible to damage before it freezes.

Snow

Watch, too, for snow damage. Plants which have become leggy and weak are especially prone to losing branches under the weight of snow. Sometimes a plant with a solid canopy, such as a rhododendron, will permit so much snow to settle on it that the whole things keels over, like a ship with ice on its rigging. If you think this is a danger, be prepared to go out in the snow and shake the plants until the crust of snow is mostly shed. Do it before the snow begins to thaw, since partially thawed snow can then refreeze, as ice and snow, on the branches, and it is then impossible to dislodge. Subsequent snows make the weight a real killer.

Good housekeeping

There are other more minor forms of garden first aid which, if less dramatic, are just as beneficial in the long term. It is always worth clearing up builders' rubbish from the garden as early as you can. Bricks under lawn mowers do serious damage, and so does the classic builders' billet-doux, the scaffolding clip; and caustic cement on leaves and soil can kill, sooner or later.

Keeping on top of the weeds

Never let the problem weeds seed in your garden. Even if you are busy with major projects, taking out trees or re-laying paths, just spend a few minutes making sure that the serious weeds such as bindweed and ground elder cannot seed. You may not have time to be digging them out or poisoning them yet, but at least you can stop them from spreading. Just pulling the tops off every few weeks is all that is necessary, or running a strimmer over them. Where you allow no flowers to open, there will be no seed to follow, while removing the leaves prevents the root system from building up strength.

It is easy to worry too soon about lawn quality unless it needs draining. Most lawns can wait until last. But it pays to stop unwanted lawn weeds seeding themselves absolutely everywhere.

There is nothing wrong with moss. It is green and even, needs no cutting and is lovely to walk on, although quite fragile. If a lawn is as mossy as this, maybe it is not the place to have grass?

Timing

Periodically all gardens get to the stage where a good deal of the structure planting needs replacement. Hedges become old and tired. Trees and shrubs get out of scale. Paths are narrowed by the gradual encroachment of shrubs. And while it would be perfectly possible to push on and do all the major clearance and heavy pruning at the beginning of the rejuvenation work, there can be virtue in saving some of the clearance until later. Especially when the clearance opens up the garden too much and too fast. So what can wait for a year or two?

Internal boundaries

Think hard about removing any internal division in the early stages. Compare the process to renovating a house. Would you remove at the start an internal wall in a house intended to be open-plan, or would you do all major works to one room first, and contain the mess in that room, until you were ready to break through? It is no fun living in a house that is a mess from top to bottom. Waiting, and doing things gradually can be a useful trick.

Even if the internal division is a scrappy old hedge or a congested shrubbery, keeping it for a few more years will allow you to enjoy the different character of the areas on either side of it. It will keep alive the element of surprise in the garden. Then, when the planting in the separate areas is re-established and interesting again, and you can enjoy being there, then you can get to work on the internal boundary.

Suppose for example you have a curving lawn with a deep border backed by a straggling evergreen shrubbery, and behind that a curving, secluded path under trees. The best way forward might be to deal first with any major tree surgery, and then re-

Double boundary plantings are extremely useful. If necessary you can cut down and regrow them one at a time, without ever losing protection within.

establish the border. When there are tall herbaceous plants thriving in the border once again, and closing the view to eye-height, then might be the time to prune back the shrubs that line the path. The prunings can brought out along the path, and the pruning need not interfere with the new herbaceous planting. In this way it is possible to keep the path's feeling of seclusion throughout the whole rejuvenation process. Making the most of a garden's character – or different characters – is what any rejuvenation is about. To sacrifice any part of that character before you need to do so is an unnecessary loss.

Maintaining seclusion

Eye-height is a magical point in any garden. If cover can be maintained to that level, even by the flimsiest of screens, then it is possible for areas of completely different character to coexist side by side. Whatever is out of sight is also out of mind.

Suppose you have repaired a terrace outside the house and established an empty bed beyond it, but the rest of the garden is going to be a building site for another 12 months. With tall annual and perennial sunflowers, dahlias, cosmos and sweet peas you might fill the beds near the terrace until it was completely cocooned in lush foliage and flowers. It could be its own private world after midsummer, and would give that longed-for effect of being in amongst the flowers themselves. Add a few pots and you would feel as if that part of the garden, at least, had been finished for years.

The key to deciding whether to delay the removal or rejuvenation of structural planting has to be the ease and convenience with which that element can be removed later. If the layout of the garden makes this easy, then time is on your

Internal hedges are invaluable for dividing a garden into separate areas. But they must be eye-height to function in this way.

Opening up a view where there was none before is best done gradually. Open a keyhole and see what you think. You may wish to adjust it left or right, or keep it tiny.

side – time to keep that leprous but not undignified old hedge across the garden for five or six years longer, until the screen planting at the bottom of the garden is established. Time to keep that oppressive cypress at least until the shelter planting on the windward side is growing hard.

On the other hand, if removing a tree or cutting back a hedge later is going to cause damage to parts of the garden that have already been repaired and replanted, then you must bite the bullet and clear it at the start.

Trial vistas

If spaces within a garden separated by a screen are eventually to be amalgamated by taking the screen away, then it is sometimes helpful to do as has been suggested, to work on the two areas separately and keep the screen temporarily, but also to clear a gap in the screen, to eye-height, so you can get used to the new vista. Seeing it regularly may suggest other possibilities which you could not have imagined on a paper sketch. If the screen is to be removed in spring, why not make a gap in it the previous autumn, so you can have the winter to consider the results and further possibilities of your future clearance? Take your time. Then, having reached your conclusion, be ruthless with the saw. Do not let the gradual approach be the route to indecision. Make it the garden you really want, not the one you have become accustomed to.

The old dowager mulberry (overleaf) has been developed as the focus of the garden, with a petticoat of clipped box and a surgical support.

Clearance

At last you have decided what is for the chop and where you are going to begin. Armed with a copious supply of energy and enthusiasm, you take out your tools – saws, axes and loppers – and your camera.

'Before and after' pictures

Although it may seem irrelevant, the first thing to do when you are ready to start clearing is to take lots of pictures. It is your last chance to record for your future satisfaction just what the garden was like before you worked on it. Photographing neglected gardens is not easy, because everything looks like a muddle. The pictures are usually unremarkable, because what you see is sheer chaos rather than an obscured design. But stand where you think the major views of the garden will be and photograph them now, even if all there is to be seen is a wall of laurel. The contrast will be all the more telling. Go upstairs and take some pictures from above. Take some from across the street or from a neighbour's garden. I promise you, if you do not take plenty of pictures now you will regret it. No one ever takes enough at this stage.

Clearing paths and open spaces

Once that is done, the hard work can start. Begin by removing those plants that you know will definitely have to go from access routes around the garden. It is really just a matter of making life easy for yourself. If you are going to be dragging branches to a chipper or a bonfire, then it will cost you a lot less effort if you can do so without having to negotiate your way around some vicious berberis that is going to be cut down anyway.

Clear the future open spaces too. This will give you room to work in, and somewhere to stack your prunings until you can deal with them. In a space which may now be a shrubbery, but which you know is going to be open lawn, you can hack away with abandon and make enormously fast progress. The thrill of seeing some open space emerge is terrific. It is extremely therapeutic, like ripping off long sheets of ugly wallpaper in an old house.

With the open spaces cleared, and major clearance of woody plants complete, then comes the time to undertake earth-moving operations, drainage and new ponds.

Major clearance always proceeds with satisfying speed. Clear paths and open spaces first, so you have room to work efficiently.

Large, overgrown laurels can be cut to the ground and regrown into a hedge this size in 4–5 years. Nip out regularly to keep bushy.

Hedges

Pruning back hedges can be a major part of any clearance and there are always large volumes of waste to be disposed of. This may be a good time to tackle them, while there is so much other waste to be dealt with. But smaller hedges can be left until the general pruning stage (page 74). Waiting gives you time to change your mind if you wish: it is not uncommon to let half-decent hedges wait a couple of years for their major pruning, until the garden has begun to recover from the first upheaval.

Bonfires

You need to decide how to dispose of all the prunings and wood you will produce. It may be that in the country you can have a bonfire in an open spot and dispose of the lot quickly and easily. Doing this allows you space to get back to the job speedily. Either have a fire burning as you cut and put the branches straight on to it or stack the material in tidy heaps containing material of similar thicknesses. This will make life easier when it comes to lighting a fire later, and you will be less inconvenienced by tangled sprawling heaps in the interim.

Remember not to set light to a heap of prunings that has been on the spot for some time without moving it to a new site. The undisturbed branches may have been chosen as shelter by all sorts of helpful creatures like slow-worms and hedgehogs.

Finding a use for the timber

But there are alternatives to burning. Trunks and major limbs of ornamental trees can be a splendid source of desirable and unusual timbers. If you have enough to be worth the cost of collecting, a timber merchant may be interested in giving you a price for the wood. It is much more likely that you will only have enough to interest a local craftsmen. People are always on the look-out for laburnum, box, walnut and yew. Some craftsmen love the chance to work in a timber new to them – perhaps the pale, light wood of a Judas tree, or the heavy, tight-grained olive-family wood of phillyrea. Find out if there is anyone in the neighbourhood who would like to take the timber. You may not get any money for it, as it will be green timber and not ready to use until it has been stored and seasoned, but at least it is going to a good home. Beware of the

All very romantic, but if the shed has got to go to the skip, it's got to go. Cut back the roses until you decide what to do with them.

person who vaguely offers to take it but never turns up, while you are left with the logs seasoning on your land and in your way. Don't pussy-foot around with people who will not take the wood away quickly. You will regret it.

There may be wood too which has little or no value – trunks perhaps of cypresses, green and full of resin which even as domestic firewood would spit horribly. These may be the ones to burn, unless you think you might have a use for them later as rustic poles. Remember only that untreated softwoods do not last well and using them in construction of hard landscaping may not be an economy in the long term. But as path edgings in a woodland garden they could be fine, and a real saving. Birch logs look most attractive as an edging because of their pale bark, which stays on the logs for a reasonable period. Some bark, such as that of sycamore, shrinks away in only a couple of months and cracks off, leaving the bare timber below.

The twiggier branches can also have their uses, as plant supports for the short-term climbers like sweet peas that you plant for instant screens. A tracery of branches built into a makeshift fence will not last indefinitely, but may be there acting as protection and a temporary visual barrier just long enough for you to see your new hedging plants established.

Using shredders and chippers

Even the twiggier prunings can be used if you have a mind to. By hiring a shredder when you have a decent-sized heap ready, you

An unwanted Lawson cypress can go three ways: stump to the bonfire, twigs shredded for recycling, and use the trunk for a prop.

can reduce twigs and small branches to chips for surfacing woodland paths or for mulching around the base of newly planted trees and shrubs. The smallest domestic machines would make heavy weather of disposing of the branches of say, an old apple tree or a Leyland cypress. But some of the larger machines would steadily gobble most of it up and leave you with a sizeable heap of chips. These could then be used straight away if the need is there – to surface an informal woodland path, for example. Otherwise, store them in a heap and allow the chippings to begin gentle decomposition until they are needed.

Thinning out trees and shrubs

With the open spaces cleared and paths all accessible, you can then begin the slower process of clearing the unwanted plants from amongst those plants which must remain. This takes far longer because you cannot just chop away with no risk of damaging other plants. It is an unpicking process.

It pays now to have really thought about what you want to achieve, because once you go cutting into an old shrubbery or woodland, there will be all manner of surprises. You may think you want to give breathing space to that blue cedar you can see poking its head out of the seedling ash and sycamores. But what if, having cut away everything around it, you find the tree is in reality spoiled beyond saving? You therefore need to cut very warily into old congested plantings, whether they are head-high or house-high.

Start with the plants which are indisputably weeds and which must go. Seedling elders, perhaps, and seedling thorn trees, and brambles. Pull them all out and get rid of them. Now you can work in comfort and begin to see the quality of the plants that remain. Now the dog can see the rabbit.

If there are other trees worthy of keeping near the cedar, fight your way into the middle of the jungle and look hard at them all. Are there trunks showing signs of rot or damage at the base, signalling that the tree is on its way out? Are that golden cypress and holly so shaded out at the base that, even if you cleared them, they would always look bald and bare in their lower parts, and certainly to above eye-height? Would it be better to sacrifice the misshapen cedar and keep the seedling ash tree for a few years, because it is at least healthy, shapely and likely to live? The art of unpicking is to make the best of a bad lot and still get most of what you want out of it. Some plants recover well from being smothered, but others are never the same again. Use Pruning to Rejuvenate (pages 97–145) to explore the prospects for your particular plants.

CLEARING TREE STUMPS

A word of warning on clearing trees. It is always better to get the stump out, so you do not encourage honey fungus, and so that replanting is not physically restricted by a cubic metre full of wood and roots. To get the stump out easily, even of trees only 10–15cm (4–6in) in diameter, it is far better to cut off the trunk no lower than waist high, so you have something to lever on when you have cut through the main roots. A stump in the ground with no trunk at all is a real pig of a job to get out.

Larger trunks with a diameter of up to 30–50cm (12–20in) may also be cut down to this height, and a winch hired with which to pull them out after the roots have been cut. Winches are dangerous tools to use, because of the tensions involved, and it is of course necessary to have something to pull against – a very well protected mature tree, for example. But they definitely make light work of removing stumps which are too big to dig out, but not so large that you wish to have the stump mechanically ground down. Most people prefer to have stumps winched out professionally.

Remove large branches while the sap is down. When removing seedling trees and shrubs, watch out that you do not hack through major roots of nearby permanent plants.

Stump grinding

Stump grinding is another job for the professional. These machines, now made narrow enough to pass through a small gate, work rather like big chainsaws. Levering against a stationary set of wheels, the toothed blade rips away at the wood left in the ground until there is nothing left within 30–60cm (12–24in) of the surface. It is rare that a grinder gets the whole stump out, and much of the buttress roots may be left behind, but it is better than having a wooden platform left in the garden. You can certainly put turf or herbaceous plants over the stump, although you would not plant another tree there.

Grinding out a stump a metre across may take half a day, and older stumps which have been dead for some time but are not rotten will take even longer. The noise is horrendous. Inadequately screened machines can put out windows and chip the paint of cars with flying stones. But afterwards when the space is clear you will not regret having had it done. You will never know the tree was there.

Killing stumps

Occasionally, with trees like willows and members of the plum and cherry family, cutting the trunk down to a stump is not enough, and suckering shoots will surface for some time from roots remaining in the ground, eventually replacing their problem parent. In these cases it is advisable to kill the stump chemically to prevent regeneration. If you find yourself in this situation, seek advice from your garden supplier on the most suitable product, and follow the manufacturer's instructions. Remember, chemical stump killers work best on freshly cut stumps. Don't wait and act a month later.

Eradicating Weeds

Pruning back trees and shrubs may cost a great deal of effort, but ironically it is always easier than dealing with pernicious colonizing weeds like brambles, bindweed and ground elder. It involves time and patience to deal with these, and the sooner you start the better, whether the intention is to work with chemicals or without.

Where to leave well alone

It may be that you are happy to live with a very wild look in the outer parts of the garden, and to plant tough herbaceous plants and bulbs in the rough, where they will have to compete with grass and 'weeds' like thistles and nettles (both beneficial to wildlife). But the likelihood is that, nearer a house, you will wish to have more controlled plantings, where rampant weeds are not constantly muddling the effect.

What is a weed?

Let's be clear what is meant by a weed. It is certainly not every less-than-spectacular native plant. Some say a weed is merely a plant in the wrong place, whether it is bracken or some specialist nursery's darling from Yunnan. But for the purposes of garden restoration, perhaps we may define the worst weeds as perennials with running roots which will seriously infiltrate other plants, and which are not easily overcome by chemicals. Annual and tap-rooted weeds (or garden plants in the wrong place) are a nuisance, but

Creeping perennial weeds: bindweed and ground elder.

they can be dealt with easily enough using a hoe. Perennial creeping weeds can smother shrubs and herbaceous plants, reducing the carefully contrived arrangement of garden plants to a rolling mass of the same generalized vegetation. The only satisfactory way to replant here is to clean the ground of weeds first.

Serious infestations

What do you do with an old mixed border riddled with something like ground elder? If the border is to be put down to grass, or you intend not to grow herbaceous plants any more, then there is no great problem. The border can be cleared, dug over, the worst of the weed roots removed and the area seeded. Any regrowth will succumb to regular mowing.

Where you cannot dig, regular spot treatment of recurring weeds using a sprayer will gradually finish them off.

But if you want to keep the area as a border, the job is much harder. One option is to keep the border empty for a couple of years, while you eradicate the weeds, and then to put in new clean plants. Another option is to dig up the herbaceous plants and divide them into pieces small enough for you to ensure there is no scrap of weed root left in there. These offsets are planted elsewhere in weed-free soil, or perhaps a bed newly dug from lawn (usually be free of weeds), until such time as you have dealt with the weeds in the original bed. The shrubs in the border will need to be pruned upwards a little, without ruining the long-term shape, so that you can get at the weeds underneath. Shrubs with fast-growing upright branch structures like roses, philadelphus and lilac will always fill out again low down. But it would not do to cut a fringe off the bottom of small, slow-growing rhododendrons, dwarf conifers or daphnes. Once the shrubs, as well as the spaces between, are free of weeds, then the herbaceous plants can come back from sanctuary and the border be reinstated.

Chemical versus organic methods

Ask yourself whether you wish to use pesticides in the garden. There is no doubt that in dealing with a neglected garden chemicals make things much easier and faster. It may be, even if you intend to maintain the garden on an organic basis later, that you are prepared to use minimal amounts of chemicals during rejuvenation, precisely so that you can cope organically later. Some would say this is a fudge. 'Oh Lord, make me good ... but not yet!' as St. Augustine said. Others would call it a reasonable compromise and a proper use of science.

'Pesticide' has become a dirty and emotive word today. It is a legislator's convenience word, used to include all garden chemicals – selective and non-selective herbicides, insecticides, molluscicides and fungicides. It is probably fair to say that the least generally harmful of these chemicals are the modern safety-approved non-selective herbicides available on the amateur market. The most useful in cleaning up a garden, and least problematic of these, is glyphosate.

Using the minimum necessary

In garden restoration there is rarely cause to spray large areas, because you are always working in and amongst plants which must not be sprayed. Almost every time, what is required is spot-treatment, putting the chemical in small amounts only on the intended plants. This is as it should be – a proper, considered and minimal use of the least harmful chemicals.

A rubber glove can be used to apply systemic herbicides.

The Green approach

If you decide to use no chemicals, there are still many ways of getting pernicious weeds under control.

Defoliation is a most potent method. In dry climates, bracken can be eradicated by cutting it off for three seasons in succession when the stems are about 60cm (24in) high, just as the side-fronds begin to expand. Ground elder can be starved into submission by constant defoliation by hand or by a lawn mower. Defoliation must be constant and rigorous, and the plant given no opportunity to expand any leaves and thus make energy from photosynthesis. It takes great dedication and attention to detail, but it is possible. Of course, if every bit of greenery is removed there will be no flowers and therefore no seedlings, except from seed which may blow in from elsewhere. Nevertheless, every little helps.

The same starvation from lack of light can be achieved over larger open areas by laying down black, light-proof polythene for a couple of seasons. It must be weighted down at the edges or dug into the soil, so no light can enter below.

Digging

However, before any attempt is made to eradicate weeds by starvation and defoliation, a first attack must be made with a fork and with a will. This applies to gardeners using chemicals just as much as to organic gardeners. There is no point in attacking a plant when it is in a position of strength and has been growing in uncontrolled abundance for several years. Dig out and burn all the root you can before you start to defoliate the regrowth. Of course, this is not easy in a densely planted border, and you will have to resort to the same system of removing plants to the sanctuary of clean soil while the dirty war is waged in the borders.

Improved drainage

Another tool for organic and inorganic gardeners is the alteration of the nature of the soil. Horsetail (*Equisetum*) is one of the hardest weeds to deal with, and grows from very deep roots indeed. But it has a marked preference for moist soils. If you can manage to improve the drainage to a considerable depth, by installing deep land drains, you will then begin to have the upper hand in the battle.

Applying chemicals

The time to use chemicals is after you have used the simple and necessary mechanical controls first. There is no point, for instance, in throwing brushwood killer at a patch of woody brambles. Kick it while it is down. Dig out as much of the weed as possible first and weaken it. Spray only the regrowth that comes from the bits of root you will inevitably have left behind. You will use far less chemical and what you do use will be more effective.

Timing

Different chemicals work in different ways. There are old-fashioned total weedkillers like sodium chlorate, which dissolves in the soil and kills everything, trees included, wherever it reaches, for two seasons at least. It can leach away from the point of application to kill plants elsewhere. The kindest chemicals to use are those systemic herbicides which can be applied carefully to the leaves of the intended victim only, and which quickly become inactive in the soil. Glyphosate and glufosinate ammonium work this way. Glyphosate is the tougher of the two, and there are virtually no plants which cannot be killed by it.

But systemic herbicides, whether applied to herbaceous or to woody plants, can only work when there are leaves there to absorb the chemical. So every opportunity to use the chemical effectively must be taken. Glyphosate works best on plants in active growth, when there are plenty of new leaves to absorb it. For the less problematic weeds, late spring is the best time to apply glyphosate. Tougher weeds, like Japanese knotweed and bindweed, which shoot exceptionally hard in the spring, are better treated in late summer. At this time of the year the chemical is translocated to the roots far better.

But one treatment does not mean to say you can then forget about the problem. Reapply the chemical as often as you see any regrowth. If the season is horribly dry, water the area to provoke some regrowth. Put on a little sulphate of ammonia, as a quick fix of nitrogen, to make the weed throw up some leaves for poisoning. The weed will suffer more from the herbicide than it gains from regrowth. In fact, you exhaust the root all the more by forcing it into growth which is not then allowed to make new energy from daylight. It's a cruel business, but worth the effort.

Getting the chemical into the plant

Often people claim that glyphosate has not worked because one application has not produced a complete kill. Plants, like animals, and like the monsters in sci-fi thrillers, are often capable of jumping up again just as you think it is safe to go back into the water. It does not mean to say that you have achieved nothing with the weedkiller, only that a coup de grâce is still required to finish it off.

Often, too, people think the chemical has not worked when in fact it has not entered the plant at all. Plants with shiny, scaly or waxy leaves – say acanthus or horsetail – will happily repel most of the spray droplets which fall on them and remain unscathed. It is necessary to break the surface of the foliage to admit the chemical. Horsetail can usefully be bruised by thwacking it with a stick before spraying. Acanthus may have the chemical rubbed into the leaves using a rubber glove dipped into a strong solution.

The glove technique is particularly useful when you need to apply chemicals to a few leaves growing in amongst a desirable ornamental plant. Under shrubs, chemicals can be applied to leaves using a sprayer lance under virtually no pressure, so that the solution barely trickles out on to the leaf you want to kill.

Where a climbing weed like bindweed has infiltrated clumps of perennials, the stems may be encouraged to climb up long garden canes inserted into the clump. The bindweed leaves can then be rubbed with a rubber glove dipped in the spray solution, if you are careful, without any chemical at all falling on the important plants.

PROBLEM WEEDS

N.B. Most pernicious weeds have glossy, scaly or waxy foliage whose surface repels water-based chemicals. To improve absorption, always use the chemical with an approved adjuvant. This may come in the form of a standard detergent to reduce surface tension in the water droplets, or in something which chemically helps the solution to penetrate the surface of the leaf, such as amorphous silicon dioxide (sold as Speed Up).

Bindweed

(*Calystegia sepium*)
Bindweed is truly a problem weed. However beautiful those white bell-shaped flowers, it will scramble through shrubs and hedges, twining its way up herbaceous plants, smothering and pulling them down with its weight. It seeds as well as running underground.

The root is white, fat, brittle and deep, and confusingly like the root of that prized ornamental climber *Tropaeolum speciosum*. Every broken bit grows, and digging it out is rarely very successful.

The best way to get glyphosate into the plant is to put tall canes into borders or alongside hedges where it grows, and to train the young shoots up the canes early in the season. Then, when there is plenty of growth on the canes, the chemical can be applied to the leaves using a rubber glove, rubbing the leaves between forefinger and thumb to ensure it gets into the leaves and green stems. You may wish to put a plastic 'bib' around the canes, to prevent any chemical splashing on to more important plants below.

Bindweed at the edges of borders can have its supporting canes eased out of the ground and be laid down on the path or lawn, on a sheet of plastic, so that the foliage can be sprayed more copiously, or dipped in a can of weedkiller. Rubbing and bruising is still important for good penetration.

Choose a time well into the season but before the plant has had time to flower and set seed. Spraying later in the season encourages the chemical to be drawn down into the root and produces a more effective kill. Spraying very early in the season tends to kill the top but produce a proliferation of buds below ground ready to rise again; early spraying is not entirely a waste, but it is less effective than later spraying.

Japanese Knotweed

(Fallopia japonica [Polygonum cuspidatum])

However dramatic and attractive this plant can be, in the wrong place it is the most difficult of weeds. It grows in dense colonies, rising to 3m (10ft) every year, and has powerful questing roots which will spear up through tarmac. It looks and behaves rather like the most rampant of bamboos, and indeed weed bamboos can be eradicated using the same techniques. Both prefer a moist soil, but will survive and still be persistent in drier ones. Eradication takes time and patience.

As much root as possible should be dug out deeply and burnt first, in winter. Chemical treatment should be saved for the regrowth over subsequent summers. Allow the stems to develop fully and then rub the leaves with glyphosate on a rubber glove. It is also helpful to cut the top off the stems and put some of the chemical mixture into the stems.

I once met someone who had had a variegated and well-behaved form of Japanese knotweed on a river bank for years. She claimed it stayed put quite happily and always maintained its substantially white foliage, and was therefore short of chlorophyll and the necessary energy to take over the garden. We went to look at the patch. It was lovely. Fine, variegated leaves on a plant only 1.5m (5ft) tall. And then we noticed a green stem here and a green stem there! It had never done this before, but you can bet your life its days of quiescence were over. Never trust Japanese knotweed.

Horsetail

(Equisetum spp.)

Horsetail is usually a weed of moist soils, and improved drainage to a considerable depth will, where practicable, help to control it. It has a deep root system and if the soil is moist deep down, no amount of surface drainage alone will suppress it.

First dig out as much root as you can, in winter. Beds of useful plants infested with horsetail may need to be emptied, and the plants broken up until they are small enough to be absolutely clean of horsetail. They can then be planted elsewhere until the space is clean.

Regrowth can then be sprayed with glyphosate when fully developed in summer. With a stout bamboo cane, thwack and swish the stems, not smashing or breaking them, but bruising the foliage, so that when you then spray, the chemical can get past the plant's scaly skin and into its system. Several treatments will be required, because all the regrowth will not appear at once.

Ground Elder

(Aegopodium podagraria)

Ground elder has two powerful means of spreading. Not only does it run underground, but it also has the ability common to all the cow parsley family, the Umbelliferae, to produce masses of viable seed. Never let it seed if you want to conquer it. Pulling off the heads as they open will do the trick, and is well worth the effort. Even people who grow the variegated ground elder as an ornamental always dead-head it to stop it seeding around plain green.

Left to its own devices, ground elder is a fairly shallow runner. Its white stems will be found just a couple of centimetres under the surface, but

whenever it stops to make a little crown of leaf it puts down a vertical tap root. Digging should always be the first method of attack. But be careful to make the most of that first attack, and to clean up all you can. For every bit of root left behind, vertical or horizontal, will sprout again in six to eighteen months. Do not think regrowth will all appear conveniently at the same moment.

Spraying of established ground elder colonies with glyphosate is more effective in midsummer when the foliage is mature. But regrowth is better hit (or redug) just as soon as there is enough leaf to take up the chemical. Defoliation alone will in the end kill ground elder (it cannot survive close mowing) and so regrowth should be given no chance to nourish its roots from sunlight for long.

Where ground elder has run into clumps of perennials, the clumps should be lifted at the appropriate time of year and broken up small enough to be able to clean them entirely of ground elder root. Replant the pieces in clean soil until the infested bed itself has been cleaned of ground elder.

Shrubs whose roots are riddled with ground elder cannot easily be cleaned of it, and will require regular spraying of the ground elder leaves (or rubbing with a dipped rubber glove) for as long as it continues to appear. Do not give it time to develop mature foliage before spraying, since this also gives it time to run out again into the surrounding clean soil.

When spraying in amongst the base of a shrub in full leaf, use a pre-pressurized sprayer on absolutely minimal pressure, so you can just dribble the chemical solution on to the weed leaves, without spray drift hitting the foliage of the shrub itself.

Bracken

(Pteridium aquilinum)

In gardens at least, bracken need not be a serious problem It is in reality just a fern with a running rootstock. As large ferns go, it is a very light-hungry species, and defoliation alone will kill it over a period of three to four years, without resort to chemicals.

Cut the bracken stems off at ground level – not when they first appear, but when the stems have risen strongly to perhaps 60cm (24in) and the side fronds are about to expand. Cutting at this moment means the plant has wasted its energy on making stems before it can store new energy from its developing fronds. The plant is thus exhausted. Digging of course can help too, but defoliation is almost as effective and far easier.

Always use a knife to cut bracken. Its stems contain silicone and can cut hands sliding along the stems.

Clearing Old Hard Landscaping

Once you have opened up the garden enough to be able to have easy access around it, the time has come to work on removing any bulky, old, hard landscaping. Now you have space, you can barrow materials from A to B with ease, but in the knowledge that things are still a mess and you are not going to be doing any harm.

Clearing the junk

Items for disposal could be anything at all. An old shed, greenhouse or concrete garage perhaps, or cracked and broken paving from an old terrace or steps. A heap of bottles from circa 1920. Two dead mowers and a broken garden roller.

Getting these items of junk out of the way will open up even more space, and highlight for you further questions. Maybe the base of the garage is concrete 30cm (12in) thick; can you really face removing it, or will you make a virtue of necessity and reuse it somehow? Maybe the garage's removal opens up a gap you are anxious to screen quickly, or one you would like to retain and develop. Maybe the terrace was in a mess because it never had any proper foundations, and you will

An old shed usually contains enough timber to construct a recycled compost bin or two.

therefore have to rebuild right from the bottom up. Maybe you will discover that collapsed shed down the garden has been an outside toilet and has a useful plumbed-in water supply.

Fences

It is a good idea to get boundary fences and gates repaired or replaced, once you are past the stage of needing to fell trees or drop branches over them, and know you have all the width of access you require for machinery. Fences with only very little life left in them are best replaced early on too, so that you can plant close up to them in safety, sure that you will not need to be wading in there to erect a new fence in a couple of years. A sound fence can then have any necessary rabbit-proofing net permanently attached to it too. Rotten wood from old fences can go on the bonfire with your tree prunings.

Recycling

Be careful that you do not dispose of any potentially useful materials too soon. It may be that some old timber will be required to make shuttering for foundations for new steps, or that a big sheet of plywood could be just the job for mixing cement on. Old planks come in useful for laying down on a lawn where you need to make repeated journeys with a wheelbarrow over the grass in wet weather. There might be enough wood to make some compost bins later, so stack anything useful somewhere out of the way, until you are sure it is not needed.

If you have rubble to spare, lose it under the foundations of paths. This will save you the cost of sending the rubble to land-fill.

Do I need to hire a skip?

Governments today are keen to reduce landfill and make considerable charges for sending waste to landfill sites. So if any old building materials can be reused on site, so much the better and cheaper. For instance, new steps, paving, walls and paths will all need soil to be excavated for a foundation of rubble. Why not dig out the soil to use elsewhere from places to be paved later, and put into the hole the broken-up floor of the garage, or that pile of broken bricks. Wood, glass and metal are better kept out of such mixtures, but anything solid and hard is useful. You may find that what originally looked like a skip full of waste will finally come down to a few bags of glass and iron for the dustbin men, and a bonfire. If you do decide to hire a skip, make sure you have ready everything you want to dispose of. Don't be saddled with left-over pieces of junk when it's all over.

Paths

Think hard about getting rid of old paths too soon. However poor their condition, it is better to be able to abuse them as much as you like, and to use them as a temporary working area while you are still undertaking major, messy works in the garden. You can rattle up and down old paths with a filthy muddy barrow as much as you want, and it will make life much easier than trying to barrow over bare soil (or, of course, a new path). The construction of all new hard-landscape projects needs to wait until all the messy dirty work is over. It may be tempting, while the skip is there, to put broken paving in it, or to scrape off the gravel surface into the skip. But if keeping it there for a little longer makes life easier, then wait. Maybe you could wait to hire the skip, and put everything in all in one go? Maybe you will need two skips? Think about how best to organize it.

After taking note of the structure's elements, the metal work can be saved and the wood scrapped, prior to rebuilding with new wood.

Pruning Trees and Shrubs

Once you have taken out the unwanted trees and shrubs, those that remain will need attention to get them back into shape and make them do the jobs required of them. In some cases, it may be a matter of reshaping; in others a matter of cutting them right down to be completely regrown. By looking in the Pruning to Rejuvenate section you can find out which plants will stand hard treatment and which must be treated more carefully.

Trees

There are many ways of dealing with problem trees, but remember the 'problem' is usually yours, not the tree's. The tree would much rather be left alone with no pruning, unless it is literally about to fall over.

So think first whether a tree could be left to grow naturally. Sometimes potentially large trees benefit from having been drawn up in their youth by surrounding vegetation and then only need subsequent space and light to make fine trees. The jungle has been their nurse, which they now leave behind.

Thinning and crown reduction

Other trees will require pruning, for a number of reasons. When a garden has been opened up and thinned out, new winds find their way in. Trees which relied on their neighbours for support in the wind, like a rugby scrum, suddenly find themselves out there on their own. Some will cope, but others will rock on their roots and face being uprooted in a severe gale. Evergreens especially suffer in this regard, as they carry their leaves, like wind-bearing sails, through all the winter winds and snows.

Treatment for instability in deciduous trees includes pollarding and thinning or shortening back the crown. But these are desperate measures, and alter irrevocably the shape and habit of the tree. If you take out the central leader, the chances of seeing a single trunk again are slender.

London planes happily withstand heavy pruning. Here a street tree which had had its top vertically reduced now has its upper canopy thinned.

Think hard about lifting the canopy of weeping trees. The 'standard lamp' look is most ungraceful, and the tree will always fight back.

Evergreens are even less adaptable. Most conifers cannot have their central stem removed without permanently ruining the shape and seriously shortening their life through the admission of disease. Yews, on the other hand, can withstand a great deal of pruning. Broad-leaved evergreens such as arbutus, evergreen oak and holly can have their branches thinned out and shortened a little to relieve the weight.

Crown lifting

Sometimes a tree will require pruning to let some light in beneath it. This is done by removing some of the lower, outward-pointing branches back to the trunk. Some trees, like lime and ash, respond well to this and a great deal can be achieved. But do remember that the newly light area of ground underneath will still be full of roots and therefore dry and impoverished. Remember, too, that some trees such as horse chestnut like to let their lower branches roll down low, and you may be fighting the habit of the tree to force it upwards. Over the years it will drop back again. Beware, too, of cutting back trees of a positively weeping habit such as weeping willow, weeping ash or parrotia. It is all too easy to make their crowns look like uncomfortable fringed lampshades dangling from their trunks.

Some trees, such as cherry and thorn, do not improve with cutting. Cherries tend to die back from large wounds and throw many long, sappy 'water-shoots' within the tree. Old thorns may look congested and full of twigs, but if you try to

thin them out you will only make matters worse and force out even more water-shoots; it is their habit to be densely twiggy, after all. With such trees it is better to live with the habit, unless you are prepared to continue pruning out water-shoots.

Shrubs

Most shrubs will stand far more hard pruning than you might expect. There are no absolute rules about what response to expect, although some respond much better than others. Look in Pruning to Rejuvenate for guidelines for each species.

If a generally robust species looks as if it could benefit, for whatever reason, from being cut down to the ground, then it is almost always worth trying it. Unless the plant is a great botanical rarity in need of conservation, it is in reality no more valuable than its purpose in the garden. If it is not doing its job, then what is there to lose? Cut it out, at an appropriate time. Give it all the help it needs. Water it. Feed it if necessary. And see what happens.

Ragged, gnarled old conifers such as this juniper can sometimes be turned into interesting sculptures by 'cloud pruning'.

How hard a hand do you like to give to pruning? These two vistas are really different versions of the same thing, just different styles. The romantic, meadowy version has to rely on particularly hard pruning of its lines of individual shrubs to stop it becoming vague and woolly. The formal version uses a hard, crisp surface underfoot, then softens it with a gentler treatment of the shrubs. Pruning can set the style of a garden, just as much as its level of health.

These clipped drums of yew were once like those still to be seen behind. Reduced to 'totem poles', they regrew to this stage in 10 years.

Using a gentle hand

There are some groups of shrubs which do not generally respond to hard pruning, and the most significant of these is the pea family, *Leguminosae*. It includes brooms, laburnum, colutea and caragana. The members of this group will tolerate cutting of young shoots well enough and break out again, but cuts into old wood frequently result in no shoots at all, and often lead to die-back and death.

Slow-growing shrubs also need treating with respect. Plants which rarely throw a shoot anywhere near the base as they grow older – witch hazels and many of the smooth-barked species of rhododendron – do not respond at all to being cut back hard. They need gentle cutting back to a live shoot and a gradual reshaping over several years.

Old or just frustrated?

Whatever the species to be pruned, part of its response will depend on its general age and vigour. There are times when it is better just to leave well alone, or if the plant is too ugly simply to get rid of it. You would not put a centenarian through a triple bypass operation, or tell him to take up weight-training. And if a shrub is plainly at the end of its days, its foliage thin and with very few vigorous shoots anywhere, either in the canopy or at the base, then you cannot expect it to shoot hard after

major surgery. Try to see the difference between plants which are congested, frustrated and in too much adversity to thrive, and those plants which have ground to a final halt.

Timing

Most major pruning is best done in the winter, but avoiding periods of exceptional cold. Evergreens, whose leaves are working all through the winter, should be left until the second half of the winter, so that they are not left leafless and energy-less all through the winter. That is not the way to get them to shoot hard.

Deciduous trees should have major cuts made through the winter but avoiding periods of sudden warmth, when certain species in which the sap rises early can bleed profusely. These include birch, walnut, maple and sycamore.

Light

If any plant is to rejuvenate itself it must have enough light. There is no point in cutting a shrub down hard if it has insufficient light to grow normally again afterwards. If the light is to be admitted a couple of years later, then wait until the light is there before you cut. Plants hard pruned before the light is readmitted will waste their reserves of energy trying to shoot again, but will only be able to make starved, poor growth for lack of sunlight to the foliage. You may kill them.

New basal shoots on this viburnum will not grow strong unless the top of the plant is cut back too, to let in the light.

Ripening the new shoots

The fast, soft shoots produced by hard pruning also need light to ripen them. A furious energy goes into those shoots, and they hardly know when to stop growing. Without warmth and sun to ripen the wood, you can find them still pushing hard at the tips in late autumn when the frosts arrive. This can shrivel the leaders even of hardy shrubs and lead to a congested habit. Extreme cold may kill the soft shoots of more tender species back to the ground, and in this way a year or sometimes more is wasted getting the plant re-established. If time is important, some winter protection of soft shoots may be useful just for the first couple of years.

Follow-on pruning

When a shrub has been cut down hard and has produced a crop of new shoots from the base, there are two ways of treating it subsequently. Either the strongest and best-placed shoot can be retained and all the rest cut away. Or the whole crop of shoots can be retained to make a multi-stemmed shrub.

It is wise to leave all the shoots intact at least for the first year, partly to give the plant some leaves and energy again, and partly to see for certain just which shoots are going to thrive best, or even survive. Even if you are aiming for a multi-stemmed shrub, there may however be weaker shoots which, after a couple of years, could usefully be removed at ground level again, to allow more light and air to a selection of the strongest. Shrubs like *Viburnum farreri* and philadelphus whose normal habit is to throw shoots from the base may, in response to cutting right down, produce so many shoots that they are immediately congested. Unless they are thinned out they will be spindly and poor, and will not make a useful skeleton for the regrown bush.

Where to cut?

How low is low, when you cut a shrub 'down to the ground'? It is wise to leave 4–10cm (2–4in) on anything, so that there will be dormant buds in that last bit of wood, which will now be induced to shoot.

If the cut is made too high, especially on shrubs which had more than one stem, then there will be more buds on the inward-pointing sides of those stumps. The shoots from these buds will crisscross in the centre of the new bush as they grow away, making a tangle at the heart of your new shrub. The shoots which grow around the outsides of these stumps will be the strongest because they will get most light. The inner ones will be the ones most likely to need thinning out either right away or a year or two later.

Lime trees readily accept pollarding, and can be cut back every year to the structure.

Putting in the New Structure Planting

Imagine a human being without a skeleton – a rather wobbly pyramid of flesh, in a business suit? Gardens can be the same: amorphous piles of plants, unless they have some bones, some structure upon which to hang.

Getting the bones in

The bones of a garden often consist of hard landscaping – walls, fences, steps and paths; but structure also comes from plants, in the form of hedges, specimen trees, topiary and even architectural herbaceous plants.

Gardens do not have to be markedly formal or full of stonework to have a strong structure. Even gardens with an easy cottagey style will often have a strong structure, of hedges and topiary, perhaps, flanking a central grass path to the front door. Strength, as ever, comes with simplicity of form.

It is a wonderful feeling when you begin to replant a garden, even if it is only trees and hedges and shelter. You feel as if you are on the last leg of the journey, and finally getting to the exciting part. When the structure goes in, even without any dressing of flowers or colour, the garden begins to smile again.

Shelter hedges need to go in early, to protect internal plantings.

Strategic trees such as these view-framing *Robinia* 'Frisia' should go in as early as is practical, to gain time and maximum growth.

Built or planted structure?

Whether the structure of a garden is to be built or planted, it needs to go in early on, because it is messy. It is preferable to install as much of the structure planting as you can before the hard landscaping structure, so that new paths and steps get no more rough treatment than is necessary. The less you move heavy weights up and down steps and run up and down new paths with a heavy barrow the better.

There are times of course when the hard structure must go in first. If final soil levels set by the hard landscaping remain uncertain, then you must wait to plant. You cannot plant a formal mini-avenue of mop-headed *Robinia* 'Umbraculifera' or standard roses until the level and exact position of the path between them is fixed. And they would be in the way and at risk when you were laying the paving for the path. You would not plant a rolling hedge of the large-leaved box *Buxus sempervirens* 'Rotundifolia' to flank a long run of steps until the steps and their retaining walls at the side were in place.

Trees and hedges

On the other hand, you would certainly plant new boundary hedges, or hedges which were meant to form a substantial internal division of the garden, or any large specimen trees. Anything in fact which involves digging big holes and getting large or heavy plants into the garden.

Should you decide to use any extra-heavy standard trees, they will probably come with a large containerized rootball. They will be expensive and worthy of the best soil preparation. So large tree pits need to be dug, generous enough to allow you to put plenty of well enriched soil around and under the tree. The rootball should not fit like a plug in a plug-hole just because it is 75cm (30in) across, any more than you would only prepare a hole 15cm (6in) across for a 2-litre pot. Accommodate your trees generously.

Digging tree pits

Digging tree pits can present various questions. What will you do with any excess soil? If the soil is stony, perhaps now is a convenient time to dispose of the stones, as hardcore under paths or terracing? If there is solid rock or chalk underneath, what then? If you can get the hole dug out, how will you get any stakes driven in? If there is clay, how will your expensive tree enjoy sitting in a hollow in solid clay? Is this a crazy place for a semi-mature tree, now you have seen below ground?

Trenches for hedges

The same kinds of problems appear when you take out a trench for a hedge. Do not plant hedge trees like individuals. They are going to be there for a long time, and life is going to be very competitive. So take out a deep trench and get some old compost or manure – anything with some humus in it – worked into the soil. In a newly acquired garden, you may have to buy in something to enliven the soil, for the luxury of a good compost heap is something rarely found in a neglected garden. Like the making of mulberry gin, these things take time.

Improving the soil

In a town soil ameliorants may need to come in bags from a garden centre. In the country you may be lucky enough to get a load of well-rotted manure or mushroom compost. If so, consider where it can be dumped by a vehicle, and be ready to barrow volumes of it to the trench.

Trees and hedges planted on good soil into what was previously only turf will not require a great deal of soil enrichment, and if bringing in ameliorants is difficult, then you could get away without it there. But it is always beneficial. On poor soils, and places where you have cleared old trees and shrubs, soil enrichment is vital for good establishment. Worked-out soils, full of root and with no humus in them or even any worms, will not give you speedy growth. What else will thrive where worms fear to tread?

Slow-growing structure plants such as these spruce take many years to fulfil their present function. Consider buying extra-large specimens.

New Hard Landscaping

The remarkable thing about putting in new hard landscaping in the form of steps, walls or even just paths is that suddenly clean straight lines or curves start to appear in the garden. Out of all the muddle of foliage some order begins to emerge. It is time, at this stage, for a lot more photographs.

Foundations

Whether you do the construction work yourself or hire a contractor, remember that all structures have foundations, and that digging out the void for them will produce a large amount of surplus soil or subsoil, and even stone. Even paths, when properly made with a hardcore base 12cm (5in) or deeper, will produce quite a volume of surplus soil. A contractor will need to be advised whether the useful spoil is to be kept on site or taken away. Think about where and how it might be used, for filling in other holes or for raising levels elsewhere in the garden. Flat gardens especially can be made much more interesting by a change of levels somewhere, even if it is only by 10–15cm (4–6in).

Good topsoil is precious. Keep it separate from subsoil, which is useful only as bulk for filling holes. If possible, store it in low heaps so that it doesn't become compacted and airless.

A stone seat doubles here as a retaining wall.

Try never to make formal classical features of hard landscaping out of cheap, second-hand materials. This crazy-paving roundel will probably be greatly improved and hidden by heavy planting.

Storage

Provision will have to be made for storing building materials. Especially if the house is in a town, then this needs to be where theft will not be a problem. Space will be needed, too, for mixing mortar. Even if the person loading the cement mixer is careful, the area around a mixer will become compacted and tainted with cement, so find a suitable place where the damage will matter least and can be put right afterwards.

Laying in pipes and cables

This is a good time to lay in services to the garden, if they are going to be needed. Water pipes or electricity cables can be put into trenches across lawns, or placed under the base of new paths, taking advantage of the already necessary disturbance.

There are pros and cons to both positions. A route across a lawn will allow you the easiest access to services in the future, should you ever need to dig them up again or extend them. But a lawn route will mean disturbance if there is a lawn already there and in good condition. With the best will in the world, trenches across lawns almost always settle a little and leave a niggling depression in the turf, to be fixed later.

A position under a path is more difficult and destructive to get at, but safest from forks and spades and tree stakes over the

Walls are best made of materials which suit the house or are local to it. If appropriate, a wall can be made into an ornamental feature.

Fencing and trellising is cheap and fast to erect, and can be used to separate composting and other service areas from the garden itself.

next 20 years. If you intend to plant every bit of the garden, then one day spending money to disturb a path may be preferable to disturbing precious maturing plants. With this in mind, consider that, even if you do not need water or electricity at the other end of the garden now, it may be cheaper in the long run to lay in the pipe or cable now, and just cap it off at the far end. When you can afford to build the summerhouse or water feature in a couple of years, it will be far easier and simpler.

Ponds need careful planning. Will it be concrete or a flexible butyl liner? How much spoil will there be, and where will it all go?

Here tree planting and a herbaceous understorey have been planted at the same time. If you can manage to maintain it, that's fine. You may prefer to concentrate your labour-intensive gardening nearer to the house at first, and to add such an understorey out here in a few years.

General Replanting

An empty (or nearly empty) bed of clean, well-prepared soil, deep-dug and enriched with old compost, is a sore temptation to any gardener. It is like coming down on a winter's morning and finding the world outside covered in a deep carpet of crisp snow. The temptation to make your mark upon it is almost irresistible. And as with the snow, every little mark you make upon an empty bed stands out in bold relief. There is no feeling quite like it.

Where to start?

But where to make the first mark? It would be so easy to find yourself planting all over the garden at once and making a useful impression nowhere. We have already looked at the installation of the structure planting and shelter planting. What remains now are the lesser trees, shrubs and all the herbaceous plants – the 'soft furnishings' of the garden. The best way to start this final decorative planting is to concentrate on one area at a time. Decide which areas or beds you would like to see completed first and start there.

Nine times out of ten this means starting with the formal areas around the house. Make these areas look finished and comfortable, and the whole garden will seem more established. If you cannot afford to put in all the planting you would like in the first year, you might put just the shrubs into these visually critical beds, and paper over the spaces around them for a season with easy annuals like poppies, calendulas, rudbeckias, larkspur or sunflowers.

Short-term effects

Bulbs can be a saviour in newly planted gardens. A bold planting of tulips interplanted in any new mixed border will provide a great fillip in the first year or two. Only, have a care when planting massed bulbs into the more informal parts of the garden since, until the trees and shrubs have begun to mature, massed daffodils can look as naive as cheap confectionery – all loud icing and no cake. It is better to plant delicately at first, or wait until the trees and shrubs have more substance of their own before gilding the lily.

Even if you have only one newly planted bed beside a patio or terrace, for the first summer you can help it along with a satisfying show of instant colour from well planted large pots. Use tall, substantial plants in them, like lilies, argyranthemums or daturas – things which have some volume and leaf-size, and the presence of shrubs.

One of the advantages of installing formal plantings is that you can begin to see the intended shapes and patterns even before the plants have matured and reached their final size, so a less-than-mature planting still has good effect. Its intention is clear. If you can complement the effect with temporary annuals and perennials, then you will gain a perfectly satisfactory short-term effect.

Shrub strategies

Shrubs in a formal garden may be intended for clipping, and will form a lesser level of structure planting within the garden, so these should be put in early. The longer they are in place, the sooner they will begin to fulfil their role of punctuating the flow of the softer, more colourful plants.

While you wait for new shrubs and perennials to establish and play their part, short-term effect can be gained through the generous use of pots, planted for colour and architectural foliage.

Small, internal hedges should be installed at this early stage.

There is a temptation to fill up large empty borders with shrubs, planting a group of three or more where ultimately one would do. That is a useful trick, and of course there is value in having groups of shrubs as well as singletons. But the risk is that in a modestly sized border, four years later none of your group of three plants is in exactly the right place. The rule must be to plant one of the group in the 'correct' place, and to add the others around it. It is also important to remember to take out the sacrificial members of the group before the permanent member is drawn up and smothered by its satellites.

In all but the largest borders, I prefer to plant shrubs at the final intended density, and to fill the space while they fill out with easy-come-easy-go perennials (including ground cover) or annuals. It is cheaper, and the risk of the shrubs being overcrowded is less.

Trees take time

Trees which are important to the design should always go in as soon as possible, for the sooner they start to look established and begin to cast some significant shade, the sooner the garden will begin to feel mature. There may be a vital trio of white-stemmed birches (*Betula utilis* var. *jacquemontii*) which are to sit cleanly on an open lawn. Or a weeping silver pear intended to take a seat under the arbour of its branches. The sooner plants like these go in the better. But extra 'interesting' trees intended to brighten up a dreary secondary shrubbery could always wait for a year or two.

Informal parts of the garden may even benefit from not having too much planted too soon. There is nothing sadder than seeing a large area of long grass spattered with dozens of little trees and shrubs. If you are a species-freak and arboretophile, then fine; get everything in at once. But if you simply want to garden, you can plant just a small number of strategically placed trees or shrubs for the first few years, and add to them once they are established, when the pressure to work on more intensive parts of the garden has reduced. Think about and enjoy the spaces, as well as the plants that define them.

Lawns and Fine Path Surfaces

The fine-surfacing of paths is a finishing touch in a garden. Foundations and paving will have been installed earlier, but the final surface of gravel paths is a job best left to the end, when all the mess is over.

A lawn, too, is still a finishing touch, although it may take up a considerable area in a garden. Lawns, together with paths and paving, are the spaces where people belong. And people are the final and most important addition to any garden.

If you find yourself rejuvenating a garden with a half-decent lawn, the best thing you can do is to keep off it as much as possible during the works, especially with heavy weights. Try your best not to compact the soil, and when the major works to the garden are over, the grass will spring to life as if nothing had happened.

But it is rarely so easy. More often there are areas which need to be put down to grass for the first time, and everywhere woolly edges to the existing lawns, where overgrown plants spilled out on to the grass or cast heavy shadows. Whether you use seed or turf to make the new areas of lawn, the soil will need to have been dug over and firmed back again, and a fine surface made to accept the grass.

Laying or improving a lawn is one of the last rejuvenative operations. If lawn weeds offend you, lay down high quality turf.

Bald patches of turf occur especially at the junctions of narrow paths. Cut in patch-repairs of turf in spring or autumn.

Turf transformations

The beauty of using turf is that, like laying a carpet, there are suddenly clean running lines around the garden. It defines new layouts like nothing else. It is this definition of the space, far more than the quality of the grass, that effects the transformation. So do not look at grass as some awful obligation to be endlessly worked at, rather as a hard-working foil for everything else which goes on in the garden.

Looked at in this light, turf can be preferable to seed, despite the increased cost. The effect is instant and it gives you a reasonably firm, clippable edge straight away, without the need to put in any kind of wooden edging.

Patching and invisible mending

However, with seed or turf you can only buy a small range of modern, super-efficient grass mixtures for broad, generalized purposes. It may be that you intend, in a year or two, to have a new billiard-table sward which will require complete remaking. In that case, patch the present lawn with whatever you can get hold of cheaply.

How you present your lawn is really a matter of maintenance style. Some like velvet stripes (opposite top), some like a lawn full of daisies (opposite below). Whichever texture you choose, a well-cut edge will give crisp definition to the garden. A lawn can set off a garden as a frame does a painting.

But if you have a large lawn and no intention of letting yourself in for a complete remake, then think harder about what you use to patch it. Old lawns have an individual character all of their own, regardless of whether they contain any wildflowers. If you put a strip of modern seed mixture full of macho super-grass strains around the edge, it will stand out as a repair for years, and very likely grow faster, too – just at the edge, where it shows the most.

Look at it this way. Would you patch a 100-year-old silk wall-hanging with a roll of flock from one of the Big Sheds? Be kind to the lawn. Give it a year or two to see how it grows, and what are its particular vices and virtues. Even if you want to give the lawn hard wear, do not put down a modern hard-wearing super-grass instead, or it will always outgrow the existing species in the lawn, and remain an obvious repair for ever. There is virtue instead in patching with a fine lawn seed mix, which in a

Shallow roots in lawns cannot be cut out without damage to the tree. Try letting the grass under the canopy of the tree grow longer to avoid scalping.

year or two will be invaded and overcome by self-sown existing species to give you an even sward.

The best way to speed on the invisibility of patch repairs in old lawns is to sow them with seed clipped from the existing lawn mixed with some fine turf seed, so that the local seed gets on there in good numbers straight away.

Whether to feed and weed?

When the lawn has been satisfactorily patched and is whole again, it is time to start thinking about whether you want to treat any of its text-book improprieties, such as moss, thatch or broadleaved weeds. If they do present themselves as a problem, try treating them very locally to start with, perhaps even using a rub-on gel for the broadleaved weeds. It is a pity to spray a whole lawn with selective weedkillers before you have had time to find out what (if any) attractive short-sward flowers may be there.

Clover-ridden lawn.

Speedwell in lawn.

Turf marked by a fairy ring.

Deep-rooted weeds you know to be present, such as thistles or docks, are best dealt with by spot-treatment with glyphosate, dribbled on to the individual rosettes of foliage. It may seem laborious, but it is surprising how much you can achieve this way, while avoiding blanket use of selective weedkillers.

Old lawns tend to take longer after the winter to acquire that fresh, green look of spring. This is because there is simply less nitrogen there. Feed it and you will get the greenness. But with it will come more mowing, greater grass density and fewer of the low-growing herbs. If you like the idea of a sward full of low-growing wildflowers, then avoid feeding and enjoy the diversity at the expense of instant spring greenery. If you want to perk up a lawn without feeding it, then a good mid-spring scarifying to pull out some of the dead grass will provide a sufficient tonic.

A mushrooming of toadstools

Not infrequently in gardens where there has been major work going on, a year or two after trees have been felled and large shrubs moved, toadstools will appear on the lawn. These are simply the fungi breaking down the dead roots left under the grass. Most of these fungi are harmless, and appear only at certain times of year, for a few years until the roots are consumed. Dig up the lawn and remove the roots if you wish. Or let the process run its course. Whether you try to remove every root under the lawn when you cut down the trees, or whether you dig out infected roots afterwards, it is still a disturbance of dubious value.

As you like it

In essence, then, lawns are what you make of them – what you want them to be. If you want a perfect emerald sward, then you must settle for the expense of keeping it that way. Like an expensive plain carpet, every bit of dirt is conspicuous upon it, and keeping it pristine requires greater and more regular effort. A lawn containing a mixture of low-growing wildflowers – the patterned carpet – will not cry 'Invader!' at the arrival of every new weed, and maintenance can be more relaxed and less frequent. It is an aesthetic, ecological and practical choice.

PRUNING TO REJUVENATE: A DIRECTORY

This pruning directory is here to help you understand the way plants behave in response to heavy pruning: some plants hate it and some thrive on it. Certain families like *Leguminosae* (brooms, caragana, colutea etc.) you will see do not generally respond well to hard pruning, while other families like *Oleaceae* (Fraxinus, Phillyrea, Forsythia etc.) sprout out most generously.

Think about whether a plant naturally has one or many stems from ground level. No matter how bushy it may be above ground level (Daphne or Hamamelis for example) if a plant invariably produces a single trunk and tends never to throw shoots from the base, it is unlikely to respond as well to cutting hard down into old wood.

Remember too that a plant which is starved and at the end of its useful life will respond less well to hard pruning than a plant three times its size but in full youth and vigour.

Common Aspects of Rejuvenative Pruning

Here are some examples of the commoner aspects of rejuvenative pruning. The following directory will tell you what any particular plant will stand.

Shrubs which sprout readily from the base, like this forsythia, can be cut down in winter to within 3–5cm (1–2in) of the ground to regrow, whatever their age.

Cutting hard back to within a few centimetres of the ground, and letting in the light, will stimulate strong new growth on all but the woodiest of old roses. Cut each stem to an outward-facing bud, if you can see one.

When there is a need to cut back a large tree severely, some species, such as holly, laurels, sycamore and thorn are better cut down to 3–5cm (1–2in) from the ground. Trunks left at 1–2m (3–6ft) respond far less well. Look how ready this holly is to respond at ground level to the chainsaw.

This willow tree has been cut right down to ground level with a chainsaw (coppiced) and 12 months later it has made an explosion of new stems. Equally, it would have made the same shoots high up if the trunk had been cut off at 2m (6ft) tall (pollarded). The stems can now all be recut regularly, perhaps every two to three years, or the shoots thinned by 80% and allowed to grow on.

The stems of very old climbers like this *Clematis montana*, or a wisteria or Virginia creeper, can be cut down with some success, new shoots arising from the old bark or from underground. It may take three months to see a response.

When a developing tree, like this ash, has lost its leader and produced two instead, cut out the weaker leader to ensure a strong clean stem in later life. Badly forked trunks (far right) can be prone to wind or snow damage in later life.

When a plant such as this *Hibiscus syriacus* has been overlaid and misshapen by other plants, it is better to reduce the overgrown side by pruning (see red marks) and to allow the spoiled side (right) to regenerate over the next few years. Dragging a plant upright to a stake only damages the roots.

When whole limbs of a tree or shrub have been bent or torn out of place by wind or snow, it is better to cut them off right back to the trunk, or in the case of this cypress, to the base of the trunk.

When taking off a branch, no matter what size, do not make a large cut which takes off the 'shoulder' of the branch, leaving the trunk smoothly vertical and parallel-sided (below right). It is far healthier for the plant to cut through the branch at the narrowest point just beyond the shoulder (below left). Eventually the bump left by the 'shoulder' will disappear into the expanding tree.

Abelia grandiflora 'Francis Mason'

Abelia   Caprifoliaceae
Abelia

§ Multi-stemmed shrubs
☐ Max. height: 2m (6ft)
♦ Semi-evergreen or deciduous
✽ Full sun

Abelias are easily grown shrubs valued for their long season of flower, from midsummer until the frosts. Ideally they should carry all the time a few new branches which have arisen from near ground level. Neglected specimens will have little new wood low down and a canopy arched over and heavy with old wood. Thin away the old branches by 50 percent in mid spring, to admit light to the base, and feed well. In subsequent seasons, when strong shoots have grown up from the base, the rest of the older wood may be cut away.

The commonest species, *A. grandiflora*, its yellow-leaved form 'Francis Mason', and the perfumed *A. triflora* are the hardiest kinds. *A. floribunda* and *A. schumannii* are less hardy and may benefit from cutting in late rather than mid spring.

Abies (Fir)   Pinaceae
Treat as for **Picea** (page 125)

Abutilon   Malvaceae
Abutilon

§ Single-stemmed shrub
☐ Max. height: 4–6m (13–20ft)
♦ Semi-evergreen
✽ Sun or dappled shade

Abutilon vitifolium and its hybrids are not often found in neglected gardens because they are relatively short-lived plants: six to ten years is the usual lifespan. However, they do sometimes self-seed. Growth can be as much as 2m (6ft) a year and the white mallow flowers are generously produced, making it a useful gap filler where short-term colour is required. Given shelter from tearing winds, this is a surprisingly hardy shrub. It is most often killed by wind-rock disturbing the roots and by snow, which can settle heavily on the felty, sycamore-like leaves and branches, until they snap under the weight.

Prune back snow-damaged branches in mid to late spring, cutting no further than is absolutely necessary.

Leggy specimens may be lightly pruned any time through the summer, shortening back all the branches to make the shrub

Abutilon vitifolium var. *album*

thicker. (Do remember that plants in heavier shade will always be less dense than those in sun and a breeze.) Do not cut into branches fatter than your thumb. In practice this means cutting only into the current season's growth, whose bark will still be green or grey, and scurfy, rather than brown. Always cut back to a live side-shoot. Branches left with no leaves rarely sprout again. Avoid cutting the central leading shoot if possible, as the subsequent forking makes the plant more prone to snow damage.

Abutilon vitifolium has mauve flowers and grey felted leaves and young stems. There are excellent white forms such as 'Tennant's White' and 'Veronica Tennant'. The hybrid *A.* x *suntense* has blue flowers and greener leaves and stems.

Acer   Aceraceae
Maple

§ Single-stemmed trees and shrubs
☐ Max. height: 2–20m (6–65ft)
♦ Deciduous
✽ Sun or part shade

The more vigorous and fast-growing a maple, the better it responds to hard pruning. *A. pseudoplatanus, platanoides, campestre, cappadocicum, macrophyllum, saccharinum* and *saccharum* are large trees and can be cut hard into wood 7–8cm (around 3in) across and will sprout well. Larger wounds may die back. Sap rises early in the spring and to avoid bleeding, large cuts should be made in early autumn or winter. Note that *A. cappadocicum* frequently produces suckers from the roots: cut these off if they are a problem.

More moderate in size are *Acer griseum*, the paper-bark maple, and the snake-bark maples like *A. rufinerve, davidii, capillipes* and *pensylvanicum*. These are much less happy to be pruned back hard. It is better to cut out misplaced branches altogether, readmit sufficient light, and allow time to repair their graceful, rather open structure. The vine maple *A. circinatum* and box elder *A. negundo* will stand harder pruning, but the resulting growths are often very sappy and disinclined to make a new tree.

The Japanese maples *Acer japonicum* and *A. palmatum* are slow-growing trees whose poise and balance is their charm. Pruning limbs hard back ruins this, and in any case the trees are unlikely to respond. The best approach for a misshapen tree is first to deal with the heavy shade causing the problem,

Acer japonicum 'Vitifolium'

Acer davidii

Alnus   Betulaceae
Alder

§ Single-stemmed or suckering trees
▯ Max. height: 20m (65ft)
♦ Deciduous
✻ Sun

Alders of perhaps 15 years old with trunks 40–50cm (16–20in) in diameter can successfully be cut down and coppiced. Very old specimens will sprout, but the new shoots never quite make such a good replacement. Side branches are better cut back to a live shoot than a stump.

Amelanchier   Rosaceae
Amelanchier

§ Single- or multi-stemmed small tree
▯ Max. height: 6m (20ft)
♦ Deciduous
✻ Sun or part shade

Amelanchier lamarckii, the commonest species, is a tough tree, but in too much shade it has neither good flowers nor autumn colour. The first priority for neglected specimens is to readmit light. Gentle reshaping is effective, taking out misplaced branches altogether rather than cutting back to stumps. Older trees may display sucker growth around the base of the trunk, often caused by physical damage from mowers or animals. They can be cut away or a multi-stemmed habit allowed to develop.

Alnus glutinosa

and then to remove such limbs as will give the tree a new balance in late summer. Thereafter light and time must heal.

Coral spot, *Nectria cinnabarina*, can be a seriously disfiguring or even fatal disease in maples, causing die-back even into the trunk. Large scale infection is almost impossible to treat.

Aesculus   Hippocastanaceae
Horse-chestnut, buckeye

§ Large trees and shrubs
▯ Max height: 4–30m (13–100ft)
♦ Deciduous
✻ Sun

All aesculus are trees which need full light. Shade turns them into spindly, weak, un-flowering affairs.

The common horse-chestnut is a fast-growing large tree, which seeds itself freely. The roots are shallow and gardening underneath is difficult, so think hard before keeping unwanted seedlings. Avoid taking out leaders if possible, as the resulting twin forks can be weak and prone to snow or gale damage later.

Many of the fancier aesculus are grafted and will display varying trunk girths above and below the graft. The red-flowered horse-chestnut, *A.* × *carnea*, is less vigorous than the type, and often looks pinched and tired in the growth of its canopy, even when the tree is perfectly healthy. *Aesculus* 'Erythroblastos' has coppery new shoots which require an open but sheltered position to give their best. The 'trick' aesculus is the species *A. parviflora*, which is a slow-growing, suckering shrub up to 4m (13ft) tall.

Ailanthus   Simaroubaceae
Tree of heaven

§ Suckering tree
▯ Max. height: 25m (80ft)
♦ Deciduous
✻ Sun

Ailanthus are not strong-wooded trees. Young wood is very pithy inside, and old trees with trunk damage can topple over. That said, they are wonderful trees. The bunches of orange seeds high on mature specimens in summer are most exotic, and so is the long pinnate foliage.

Cut down a healthy ailanthus and huge suckers will arise from the stump and the roots. It is tempting to cut them down just to get these suckers, straight as a die, soaring up to 10m (30ft) in four to five years with leaves a yard long. Pure jungle – but no flowers on this young wood, unfortunately.

Aralia elata in autumn

Aralia
Araliaceae

Japanese angelica

§ Spiny-stemmed suckering shrub
☐ Max. height: 4–5m (13–16ft)
♦ Deciduous
✳ Sun or part shade

What style *Aralia elata* has! The fat, blunt-ended, spiny, and little-branched stems are as statuesque in winter as the huge, 1m (3ft) long pinnate leaves are in summer. The white cones of flower come at the top, in autumn. Aralia stems occasionally become 4m (13ft) trunks 10cm (4in) or more across at the base. At this size they are often heavier than their shallow roots can support, and they fall over, so do not make plans around an old aralia trunk. The chances are it will only be there for a few more years. However, cutting down an old trunk in winter, or digging nearby and damaging the roots, will throw up more vigorous stems to replace it. Young stems are better left unpruned, although frost will sometimes spoil the leading shoots as they emerge in spring, and they then need to be cut back to the next bud to emerge.

There are flamboyant cream and yellow variegated forms of aralia (*Aralia elata* 'Variegata' and 'Aureovariegata') which are slower and more tender than the common type. They are propagated by grafting, so if you cut these fancy forms right down, or if they sucker from the roots, then the suckers will only be the common green. Shortening back to a side-shoot is therefore worthwhile in very old variegated plants, if they show signs of falling over. Old stems of all aralias tend to lean over at the top, and this does not mean that the stem itself is falling over.

Araucaria
Araucariaceae

Monkey puzzle

§ Single-stemmed conifer
☐ Max. height: 25m (80ft)
♦ Evergreen
✳ Sun

Old monkey puzzles (*Araucaria araucana*) are usually found to be bare at the base, and carrying many shabby lower branches. Shade and dryness are the usual causes. Cut off the worst branches clean to the trunk, and let light and air do what healing is possible – more a case of tidying than rejuvenation. Occasionally a side shoot is produced low down out of an old trunk, but these are curious rather than useful. If a tree has lost its leader to shade or damage from other trees, it is not worth keeping.

Arbutus
Ericaceae

Strawberry tree

§ Single-stemmed shrub or tree
☐ Max. height: 5–20m (16–65ft)
♦ Evergreen
✳ Full sun

Arbutus unedo is the hardiest species. Old specimens which may have been shaded out in part, or drawn to the light, can have whole branches removed in late winter, to help prevent the tree heaving over. Large wounds sprout remarkably well, and trunks of 10 and 20cm (4–8in), across, when cut right down in winter, will regrow to 2m (6ft) in a couple of years as a multi-stemmed shrub.

The larger species such as *A. menziesii* and *A.* x *andrachnoides* will respond to hard pruning, but it is better to prune minimally, in order to retain as much as possible of that wonderful coppery, scaly bark.

Aucuba
Aucubaceae

Spotted laurel

§ Multi-stemmed shrub
☐ Max. height: 2m (6ft)
♦ Evergreen
✳ Sun or heavy shade

Aucuba japonica is known to most of us only by its variegated form, the spotted laurel, which was introduced from Japan in 1783. It is an extraordinarily tough plant, and can be seen in old gardens still soldiering on from Victorian plantings. Unsupported, it will grow to 2m (6ft), but it will grow to half as high again where it can hoist itself into the branches of adjoining trees.

Older branches can become as much as 7cm (3in) across at the base. Heavy top-growth causes the branch to crack at ground level and fall over, where it may die or survive to layer itself down and grow up again. It is possible to find a complete ring of bushes of spotted laurel around a central stump which was the parent plant.

Overgrown bushes of aucuba can be cut as hard as you like. Shortening back old branches will temporarily improve the shape, but it rarely extends the life of the branch. It is better to cut down low part of the bush – perhaps the back, which is not seen – in late winter to develop new strong branches from the base. The next year you can follow suit with the front of the bush, until the whole plant is rejuvenated. If a plant has a great deal of dead wood and decay at the root, it may be better to dig it out and replace it with a layer if you have one. Feeding helps but is not vital.

Remember that aucuba needs male and female plants to produce berries, so do not

Aucuba japonica 'Variegata'

be too hasty to get rid of any, until you have had a season to see which is which, and which you could spare. 'Variegata' is the common female. 'Crotonifolia', with a more marked and less spotty variegation, is a common male. The new green 'Rosannie' is said to bear male and female flowers.

Azalea   Ericaceae
See under **Rhododendron** (page 130)

Bambusa   Gramineae
Bamboo

§   Clump-forming or suckering perennials
☐   Max. height: 2–7m (6–22ft)
♦   Evergreen
✻   Sun or shade

Bamboos comprise many genera including *Bambusa, Fargesia, Phyllostachys, Arundinaria, Sasa, Pleioblastus* and *Chusquea*. In the tropics they can reach the height of a large tree – quickly! – but in cool temperate climates the hardy species vary from 1–7m (3–22ft).

Bamboos divide mechanically, if not botanically, into runners and clumpers. Both

Chusquea culeou

can if necessary be cut down to the ground in spring, either for regeneration or even for access. They will come up again quickly. Fine-stemmed dwarf bamboos in particular benefit from this periodically.

The most useful bamboos in a garden are those which form clumps, and these over the years can become tired and weak, especially in root-riddled shade. Improve the light first. Then feed and mulch heavily in late spring. Cut out all the dead canes, and thin out 30 percent of the older canes too, to let in light and moisture to the clump. Once you have grown a thinned, attractive clump of bamboo, you will never again settle for a dreary congested clump, where the beauty of the individual stems cannot be appreciated.

Where running bamboos have spread through a moist garden, a great deal of heavy spade-work over many years, and perhaps chemical control (treat as for **Japanese knotweed**, page 71), will be necessary.

Berberis   Berberidaceae
Barberry

§   Multi-stemmed or suckering, spiny shrubs
☐   Max. height: 50cm–3m (2–10ft)
♦   Evergreen or deciduous
✻   Sun or partial shade

An overgrown berberis is not something to be tackled lightly. Be bold and resolute, if not bloody. Put on stout gloves, and with long-armed pruners or a chainsaw, chop the main branches back, cutting at least 60cm (2ft) inside the future outline of the shrub. Burn the prunings if you can, on a hot fire as near to the site as possible. The more you move berberis clippings around the garden, the more wheelbarrow punctures you will have and the more skin punctures when weeding. Alternatively cut the plant off at the stocking tops. It will grow again hard and fast, and can then be pruned to size or allowed full rein again. Deciduous species can be cut any time in winter, but evergreens are better left until mid spring.

Betula   Betulaceae
Birch

§   Single-stemmed trees
☐   Max. height: 10–20m (30–65ft)
♦   Deciduous
✻   Full sun

All birches, from the common silver birch *Betula pendula* to the fancy white-stemmed

Betula pendula

Betula utilis var. *jacquemontii*, are pioneer trees, which seed themselves into open ground in full sun. Shade will ruin them. Trees which have been badly shaded low down may still go on to make good trees if the leader and upper branches are undamaged.

Birches do not respond to having their branches cut back, except to look butchered and miserable. Specimens which have got too large for their position should either be removed entirely, or have a number of the branches cut out in winter, right back to the trunk, to leave a balanced tree.

Species with fancy coloured bark (*Betula utilis, nigra, albosinensis, maximowicziana*) may become green with algae and lichen where shade has enveloped them. A hose pipe and a vigorous scrubbing brush will return some colour to the trunk.

Brachyglottis Compositae

Senecio

§ Multi-stemmed shrubs
▯ Max.height: 1m (3ft)
♦ Evergreen
✳ Full sun

Brachyglottis Dunedin Group 'Sunshine' may sound like a carpet pattern, but it is in fact the new correct name for the old *Senecio* 'Sunshine', an improved variety of the even more familiar *Senecio greyi*. Names apart, this sun-loving, grey-leaved, yellow-flowered daisy bush can be cut down hard in late spring (it is better cut hard down than shortened). Old bushes eventually tire of being cut back, or get leggy, and they are better replaced with layers, which occur naturally, or by cuttings.

Buddleja Buddlejaceae

Butterfly bush

§ Multi-stemmed shrub
▯ Max. height: 4m (13ft)
♦ Mostly deciduous
✳ Full sun

The common species is *Buddleja davidii*, loved by man and butterfly alike. In old age it can make a trunk 10–20cm (4–8in) across at the base, but the flowers will be small. It is a pioneer opportunist species, happy to colonise bare waste ground. It will even seed itself into wall tops and flower there. When it is put into

Brachyglottis 'Sunshine'

Buddleja davidii

rich border soil it grows faster than ever. But softer growth means the trunk is likely to perish sooner than on lean dry soil. In neglected gardens buddlejas are very often seedlings of the original planted variety and may be poor in flower quality. *Buddleja davidii* with trunks over 10cm (4in) at the base are not worth preserving, and are better replaced by hardwood cuttings or scrapped.

Pruning to bring a wayward plant to heel and to see flower quality is done with a saw in late winter, to 1–1.2m (3–4ft). The flowers are then produced in late summer on the new season's growth, and subsequent annual pruning is done in spring.

The same rejuvenative pruning applies to the orange *Buddleja globosa*, but since it flowers on old wood, it is thereafter pruned lightly after flowering in early summer.

Buddleja alternifolia is a more tree-like species, with the habit of a small weeping willow and mauve flowers in early summer. The flowers are produced on the previous season's wood. An old specimen can become an impenetrable tangle. Do not cut it hard down, but thin it drastically in early spring, and cut out all the crossing branches to show off the weeping habit.

Buxus (Box) Buxaceae

See **Hedges** (pages 140–143)

Callicarpa Verbenaceae

Callicarpa

§ Multi-stemmed shrubs
▯ Max. height: 2m (6ft)
♦ Deciduous
✳ Sun or part shade

Tired old plants may have older stems removed low down in mid spring, leaving younger stems to fill their space. Feed and mulch well. Flowering and fruiting (purple berries) may take some time to recommence.

Callistemon Myrtaceae

Bottle brush

§ Single-stemmed shrub
▯ Max. height: 2–3m (6–10ft)
♦ Evergreen
✳ Full sun

All callistemons require full sun to thrive, and are often shaded to extinction in neglected gardens. Without human hand to pinch out the leading shoots, and without wind and air to keep them stocky, *Callistemon citrinus* becomes very gangly in a moist climate and in rich soils. Plants which have partially died out from shade, or are unacceptably gangly, should be scrapped or replaced. Cuts into old wood produce little or no response.

Callistemon

Calluna   Ericaceae

See **Heaths and Heathers** (page 139)

Calycanthus   Calycanthaceae

Treat as for **Hamamelis** (page 114)

Camellia   Theaceae

Camellia

§ Single-stemmed shrub
[] Max. height: 4–6m (13–20ft)
♦ Evergreen
✲ Sun or partial shade

When camellias have sufficient light and moisture at the root, they are capable of being cut down low with a chainsaw in early to mid spring and made to sprout again. Plants in poor dry soils find it harder. Very old trunks upwards of 15cm (6in) across may struggle to shoot again, and should either be pruned less heavily or replaced. Old heavy-limbed plants may be given a new lease of life by removing some of the branches, and thinning the remainder. This reduces the weight to stop them falling over, and allows light into the centre of the plant, to encourage new shoots. A mulch of old compost or leaf mould is most beneficial. It is even possible to cut back a healthy camellia all over in late winter, leaving it with only stumps 5cm (2in) across, virtually leafless; it will sprout again, and should flower within two years.

Caragana   Leguminosae

Pea tree

§ Single-stemmed shrub or small tree
[] Max. height: 6m (20ft)
♦ Deciduous
✲ Full sun

Caragana is in the pea family and the usual rules apply. Cutting into the current season's wood is tolerated, preferably in midsummer after flowering, but cutting into older wood induces no new growth, and may cause dieback. The tree is therefore not responsive to reshaping when it has been shaded out or has become misshapen. Such specimens should be replaced.

Carpenteria   Hydrangeaceae

Carpenteria

§ Single- or multi-stemmed shrub
[] Max. height: 3m (10ft)
♦ Evergreen
✲ Full sun

Carpenteria californica will, in a warm sheltered spot, make a large shrub. It is not responsive to hard pruning. It is better to cut out wayward branches and stabilize the shrub, leaving time and readmitted sunlight to undertake further healing.

Camellias can become huge but respond well to hard pruning.

Carpenteria californica

Carpinus   Corylaceae

Hornbeam

§ Single-stemmed tree
[] Max. height: 20m (65ft)
♦ Deciduous
✲ Sun

As a tree, hornbeam (*Carpinus betulus*) is most amenable to heavy winter pruning. It is one of the trees traditionally pollarded in England since medieval times.

The upright form 'Fastigiata' eventually makes a large, heart-shaped crown, and not the upright narrow crown usually associated with the word fastigiate. Unfortunately, pruning off the outer branches will not turn this plant into a narrow tree. The shape, attractive in itself, must be lived with for its own merits.

See also **Hedges** (pages 140–143)

Caryopteris   Verbenaceae

Caryopteris

§ Multi-stemmed shrub
[] Max. height: 1.5m (5ft)
♦ Deciduous
✲ Full sun

Caryopteris x *clandonensis* flowers on the new season's wood, and is therefore usually pruned down to a few centimetres above the ground in spring, before growth starts. Plants which have been left unpruned for many years pile up high in an arching mound, and flower size is much diminished. But they can survive like this for many years. Cut the whole bush down in early spring and feed and mulch heavily.

Cassinia   Compositae

Cassinia

§ Single-stemmed, twiggy shrub
☐ Max. height: 2m (6ft)
♦ Evergreen
❋ Full sun

Cassinia leptophylla ssp. *fulvida* is usually seen as a golden-leaved bush carrying clusters of minute white daisies. It is often planted with heathers because it requires an acid soil. It needs plenty of pinching and nipping out, especially in the early years, to make it a shapely plant. Old specimens which have become rangy like an old broom may have wayward branches shortened back. Time and light may then thicken the bush again, but cutting down low does not produce satisfactory regeneration.

Castanea   Fagaceae

Sweet chestnut, Spanish chestnut

§ Single-stemmed tree
☐ Max. height: 25m (80ft)
♦ Deciduous
❋ Sun

Castanea sativa can be hard pruned in winter and even coppiced if required. Trees can live to a great old age, and trees which look less than in their prime will soldier on for decades.

Cefrus libani ssp. libani

Ceanothus

Ceanothus   Rhamnaceae

Californian lilac

§ Single-stemmed shrub
☐ Max. height: 2–4m (6–12ft)
♦ Evergreen or deciduous
❋ Full sun

Ceanothus are not long-lived shrubs. Ten years is a long life. They require full light and warmth to thrive. Pinching out the tips of the shoots in youth makes them bushier, and this is worthwhile even when growing them on a wall. Cuts made into old wood produce no new shoots, and branches shaded out by other plants will not regenerate when light is readmitted. Regeneration does sometimes occur from the base, when the top has been killed by severe frost. Waste no effort on old and disfigured specimens, but replace them at once.

Cedrus   Pinaceae

Cedar

§ Single-stemmed conifer
☐ Max. height: 25m (80ft)
♦ Evergreen
❋ Sun

An old cedar is a fine thing. It produces unreasonably sentimental reactions. Cedars find their way into gardens where there is not space for a (relative) teenager, never mind a mature specimen.

Both the flat-branched *Cedrus libani* ssp. *libani* and the more upright and often blue *Cedrus libani* ssp. *atlantica*, have a narrow habit as young trees. After 6m (20ft) they begin to broaden and develop that huge wide, light-demanding canopy. Pruning to make the shape otherwise is not successful. So unless there is space for a cedar to spread its wings, take it out while you have the opportunity and before the heartache begins.

The deodar cedar, *Cedrus deodara*, has weeping ends to its branches, which also look uncomfortable when pruned back. Give it space or forget it.

If a young cedar loses its leader, it is worth fastening a cane splint to the replacement leader for a year or two, to ensure it continues upright at a sensible and graceful angle.

Ceratostigma Plumbaginaceae
Hardy plumbago

§ Suckering shrub
◻ Max. height: 1m (3ft)
♦ Deciduous
✳ Sun

Established plants of ceratostigma may be cut down to the ground or a few centimetres every year in late spring. The blue flowers are made on the end of the new season's wood. Plants which have not been pruned for many years may be cut right down in spring, and (just as important) fed and mulched well.

Cercis Leguminosae
Judas tree

§ Single-stemmed shrub or small tree
◻ Max. height: 6m (20ft)
♦ Deciduous
✳ Full sun

The Judas tree requires full light to thrive and flower. Light and air may be all that is required to get one flowering again. Shade will cause branches to die out. Coral-spot fungus (*Nectria cinnabarina*) can also cause considerable die-back. A few older limbs can be cut out, but regrowth is unpredictable. The tree cannot be pruned hard all over with acceptable results. Better to let a disfigured plant live out its days so long as it remains picturesque, and then remove it.

The common species *Cercis siliquastrum* is the largest hardy species. The smaller, shrubby *Cercis canadensis*, usually seen in the purple-leaved form 'Forest Pansy', rarely flowers in Britain.

Cercis **on a pergola**

Chaenomeles 'Crimson and Gold'

Chaenomeles Rosaceae
Japonica, flowering quince

§ Single-stemmed or suckering shrub
◻ Max. height: 3m (10ft)
♦ Deciduous
✳ Full sun, or dappled shade on a wall

Chaenomeles are all too willing to recover from being cut off at ground level, but a forest of thin stems appears instead of the original single one. These may need thinning to make a good new bush. Be careful when digging around chaenomeles, as damaged roots can also throw up suckers. For this reason also be careful, when removing a chaenomeles altogether, that you get out all the roots, or suckers will linger on for years.

Pruning is best carried out during the winter months, but major pruning even in summer will not kill it.

Chamaecyparis Cupressaceae
False Cypress

§ Single-stemmed conifer
◻ Max. height: 25m (80ft)
♦ Evergreen
✳ Sun

Chamaecyparis of any species (*lawsoniana* is the common one) will not reclothe themselves where a branch has been lost or shaded out until it becomes brown. With old, shabby specimens, it is a case of deciding whether you want to live with it for a little longer and see some modest improvement, or whether you would rather bite the bullet and remove it now. This applies both to the dwarf forms and to the forest trees.

Chamaecyparis lawsoniana 'Green Pillar'

Major reduction of the leader into old wood is not successful practically or aesthetically. Trees in need of drastic shortening are better replaced.

Golden forms require even more light to look their best, and will never glow in shade. Forms such as 'Elwoodii' which have parallel upright stems, can be badly sprained and torn by the weight of snow. Once sprained, they will not hold themselves up again, and spoiled specimens are better removed.

See also **Hedges** (pages 140–143)

Choisya ternata

Chimonanthus Calycanthaceae

Winter sweet

§ Single- or multi-stemmed shrub
☐ Max. height: 3m (10ft)
♦ Deciduous
✳ Full sun

A *Chimonanthus praecox* in full winter bloom is one of the sweetest smells in the garden. To make ripe flowering wood they need plenty of warmth and sun. Neglected specimens most frequently only need the removal of smothering shrubs and the readmission of light to make them flower again. It is a very long-lived shrub.

Pruning of lank and overgrown specimens is best carried out gradually, taking a few major stems down to half a metre below the desired height, and watching the response. If the plant responds well, take a few stems down to half a metre from the ground to encourage new growth lower down.

Choisya Rutaceae

Mexican orange blossom

§ Single- or multi-stemmed shrub
☐ Max. height: 3m (10ft)
♦ Evergreen
✳ Sun or part shade

In sun, and with sufficient shelter from winds or snow breakage, choisya will simply get bigger and better with age. If there is enough room for a 3m (10ft) dome, then fine. In shaded conditions they are frequently drawn towards the light and become bald at the back and it may be necessary to shorten the whole canopy to freshen it.

Pruning should be done in late spring after the frosts are over. Choisya will usually recover from cutting off at the base, but it is kinder and faster to shorten back the branches to the desired point over part of the bush, and when new foliage has been made, to continue with the rest in the next season.

Cistus Cistaceae

Sun rose

§ Single-stemmed shrub
☐ Max. height: 1–2m (3–6ft)
♦ Evergreen or semi-evergreen
✳ Full sun

Only in a hot dry situation will you find cistus in a long neglected garden. They are sun worshippers, and need good drainage to survive more than a few years in most of Britain. Where they are happy, they will self-seed. Old specimens of the taller species like *Cistus laurifolius* and *C. x cyprius* can make as much as 2m (6ft), but they usually become gaunt and straggly with it. Cuts into old wood do not produce new shoots, and pruning has to be careful, always taking back branches to good live growth, in the hope that these shoots will develop a new canopy. Really straggly plants are better dug out and replaced.

Clematis Ranunculaceae

Clematis, old man's beard

§ Climber
☐ Max. height: 3–10m (10–30ft)
♦ Deciduous and evergreen
✳ Sun or part shade

The large-flowered hybrid clematis rarely survive in seriously neglected gardens. Without sun and good feeding, and with

competition from too many roots, they slowly fade away and die. Old specimens still in reasonable health can be cut down in early spring to 50cm (2ft), fed hard, and generally shocked back into a busier life. Give them cool feet, sunshine in their faces, and plenty to eat and drink, and they soon smile again. The same goes for smaller species like *Clematis alpina* and *C. macropetala*.

Clematis montana is much more of a survivor. It can rise above the jungle of shrubs and perennial weeds, producing far from its roots a spectacular tangle of dead and live stems and birds' nests. The prospect of disentangling such a knot is most depressing, and the job is not worth the effort. Instead, chop away the head of the plant with shears, or if you prefer, a chainsaw. If possible retain two or three of last year's stems still attached, preferably ones which start from low down in the tangle. These will form the basis of a

Large-flowered clematis mix well

whole new plant. If need be, it is possible to chop through the main stem in early spring at waist high or less, even when it is 6–7cm (3in) across. Usually, though not always, a new shoot will appear, sometimes after two to three months. At this stage, it is vital to feed and water well.

Clerodendrum bungei

Clerodendrum Verbenaceae
Clerodendrum

§ Single-stemmed small tree or suckering shrub
☐ Max. height: 4m (13ft)
♦ Deciduous
✳ Full sun

The suckering, pink-flowered *Clerodendrum bungei* can be cut to the ground every year if necessary. In colder climates the weather can do this anyway. So chopping off gaunt old stems to ground level is no problem at all, and flowers reappear the next year, or if the season is hot, in the first year.

White-flowered *Clerodendrum trichotomum* is a single-stemmed shrub or small tree, and it does not respond well to hard pruning. Lower branches which may have been shaded out by competing plants will need to be removed back to the trunk, and the upper canopy allowed to spread out in their place. Very disfigured trees may be better scrapped and replaced.

Clethra Clethraceae
Sweet pepper bush

§ Single-stemmed or suckering shrubs and small trees
☐ Max. height: 2–4m (6–12ft)
♦ Deciduous
✳ Full sun

Most of the larger species of clethra are rather tender and only found in milder gardens. Tree-like species are best cleared of competing vegetation to admit light, and left to recover by themselves. Some reshaping by the removal of unbalanced branches in late spring can be beneficial.

More common and hardier is *Clethra alnifolia*, the sweet pepper bush. It is a suckering shrub, useful for its perfumed late summer flowers, and enjoys a moist acid soil. Older stems may have a heavy, bowed head, and these can be removed just above ground level in spring, to encourage a crop of new stems. Younger, healthier stems can be retained. *Clethra alnifolia* does not always carry suckers, and it may only be after hard pruning that the plant moves from a single stem to a multi-stemmed or suckering shrub. Flowers will reappear in one to two seasons.

Colutea Leguminosae
Bladder senna

§ Single-stemmed shrub
☐ Max. height: 3m (10ft)
♦ Deciduous
✳ Full sun

Like all pea-family shrubs, colutea is best managed by regular pinching to keep it bushy. It will regenerate from cuts into moderately old wood, but it cannot successfully be reduced to ground level. Lank specimens should if possible be reshaped to a lower level in late spring, always cutting back to strong live growth.

Colutea orientalis

Cornus alba 'Sibirica'

Cornus Cornaceae
Dogwood

§ Single-stemmed small trees or suckering shrubs
☐ Max. height: 6m (20ft)
♦ Deciduous
✳ Sun or part shade

The single-stemmed dogwoods are grown for the elegance of their branch structure (*Cornus alternifolia* and *controversa*) or the coloured bracts around their flowers (*Cornus kousa, florida* and *nuttallii*). These species do not respond well to major pruning, and are best gently reshaped, letting light and time do most of the healing.

The multi-stemmed dogwoods with coloured bark (*Cornus alba, stolonifera*, etc) can be cut down to the ground in late winter, whatever their age, and they will respond with a forest of strong new shoots. These can either be cut again every one to two years, or left to make a larger bush. The British native *Cornus mas*, grown for its witch hazel-like spring flowers, can also be cut to the ground to regenerate if need be, and reshaped into a large shrub.

Corylopsis   Hamamelidaceae
Corylopsis

§ Medium to large spreading shrubs
▯ Max. height: 2–3m (6–10ft)
♦ Deciduous
✳ Sun or part shade

Corylopsis are related to the witch hazels, and do not enjoy or respond well to hard pruning. Old specimens may have the dead wood removed and some branches shortened to reshape the bush in spring. Then light and time will heal.

Corylus   Corylaceae
Hazel

§ Large suckering shrub or small tree
▯ Max. height: 5–6m (15–20ft)
♦ Deciduous
✳ Sun or shade

There are a few hazels (*C. chinensis, colurna,* etc) which make spire-shaped trees with a heavy trunk. The common nut-bearing species, *Corylus avellana* and *C. maxima*, are more commonly found as multi-stemmed trees or shrubs. They can both recover very well from being cut off at ground level in winter, and this technique has been used for centuries in the production of hazel for basket making, pea sticks, etc. Old hazels, if they must be cut, are far better cut right down than cut halfway. The subsequent new growth and foliage after cutting is spectacularly lush and

Corylus maxima 'Purpurea'

Corylopsis

strong, and in the purple forms this is singularly attractive.

Remember that some of the fancy forms of hazel, such as the golden 'Aurea' and the corkscrew 'Contorta' are grafted, and so cutting them down below the graft will only produce common hazel shoots thereafter.

Cotinus   Anacardiaceae
Smoke tree

§ Single-stemmed shrub or small tree
▯ Max. height: 6m (20ft)
♦ Deciduous
✳ Full sun

Very old cotinus do not accept being cut off at ground level. It is better to shorten back and thin the branch structure, reducing weight if the bush looks likely to heave over (this is a common fate of old specimens). Branches up to thumb thickness will sprout well after cutting, but older wood becomes less and less willing. *Cotinus obovatus* makes a considerably larger plant than the more common *Cotinus coggygria* or its purple forms.

Cotoneaster   Rosaceae
Cotoneaster

§ Small trees and shrubs of all sizes
▯ Max. height: 5m (16ft)
♦ Deciduous and evergreen
✳ Sun or part shade

All but the very oldest cotoneasters will regenerate from being cut right down in spring, but those grown as standards on a trunk will not

be as good or shapely again. Prostrate and low-growing species can be sheared off at ground level and regrown if necessary. Flowering will recommence in one to two years.

Cotoneasters regenerate better from the base than from the stumps of heavy branches which, if left, frequently die back to the base anyway. Pruning back large branches can result in new shoots appearing at odd and un-useful angles.

Crataegus   Rosaceae
Thorn

§ Single-stemmed trees
▯ Max. height: 10m (30ft)
♦ Deciduous
✳ Sun

The fate of old thorns, from the common double red *Crataegus laevigata* 'Paul's Scarlet' to the distinguished *Crataegus* x *lavalleei,* is to end their lives with a crown full of dense, wiry twigs. It may look congested, and many gardeners have an urge to thin it out and let the air in. When this is done, the spaces are at once filled by a mass of rigid, soft water-shoots which look far worse. If at all possible, leave old thorns alone. They can live to 150 years or more, and like a good wine, acquire ever more character with age.

Crataegus prunifolia

Crinodendron   Elaeocarpaceae
Lantern tree

§ Single- or multi-stemmed shrub
⬚ Max. height: 6m (20ft)
♦ Evergreen
✽ Partial shade

Crinodendrons need a lime-free soil and good rainfall to thrive. They are often grown against a wall where old specimens will lean forward at the top and become bald at the base. Pruning should be gradual, shortening back some branches in late spring and completing the task the next year if the response is adequate. Cut some of the forward branches lower, to encourage new growth

Crinodendron hookerianum

low down. Younger plants can withstand having the whole plant cut down low, but older ones rarely survive this.

Cryptomeria   Taxodiaceae
Japanese cedar

§ Single-stemmed conifer
⬚ Max. height: 25m (80ft)
♦ Evergreen
✽ Sun or part shade

Like the Scots pine, *Pinus sylvestris*, *Cryptomeria japonica* is a tree whose character can distinguish itself with age. Be reluctant to take pendulous or billowing branches off old specimens, since, as time goes by they can develop their own balance and poise. There is much more to cryptomeria than an up-and-down forest conifer. Give them enough light and they will do the rest.

Cryptomeria japonica

The perpetually juvenile form of the tree, *Cryptomeria japonica* 'Elegans', is at its best when young. It refuses to make a good, strong trunk, and in age its feathery branches can pile up and fall over, like a pillar of candy floss. It is not then worth saving.

x Cupressocyparis   Cupressaceae
Leyland cypress

§ Single-stemmed conifer
⬚ Max. height: 30m (100ft)
♦ Evergreen
✽ Sun

Given space and good soil, the notoriously fast-growing conifer x *C. leylandii* is wind-firm. For details of pruning, see **Hedges** (pages 140–143).

Cupressus   Cupressaceae
Cypress

§ Single-stemmed conifers
⬚ Max. height: 25m (80ft)
♦ Evergreen
✽ Sun

The narrow blue *Cupressus arizonica* requires only good light and to be left alone. Snow- or wind-torn branches can be shortened back to the main canopy in mid spring, leaving as invisible a stump as possible.

The Monterey cypress, *C. macrocarpa*, will make a narrow column in many gardens, yellow in forms such as 'Goldcrest'. On the western coast of Ireland and France it makes a more cedar-like shape, with branches held out level or nearly so. Pruning will not turn one habit into the other.

Cytisus   Leguminosae
Broom

§ Single-stemmed shrub
⬚ Max. height: 1– 4m (3–12ft)
♦ Evergreen or deciduous
✽ Sun

Brooms are not long-lived shrubs. In neglected gardens, the chances are that any brooms are self-sown seedlings from previous plantings. Brooms quickly become straggly without an annual haircut after flowering in early summer, and they will not produce shoots from wood more than one to two years old. Cutting back hard does not work, and ugly specimens should be scrapped and replaced.

The pineapple-scented Moroccan broom, *Cytisus battandieri*, is a rather unusual member of the genus, with fatter stems and large yellow flowers. It is slightly tender and therefore often grown as a wall shrub. Top-heavy specimens can be improved by careful cutting back to strong shoots, to remove the worst of the overhang, and by making sure that light can easily get to the bottom of the plant so that any new low shoots can develop properly.

Cupressus macrocarpa

Daboecia   Ericaceae
See **Heaths and Heathers** (page 139)

Daphne   Thymeleaceae
Daphne

§   Single-stemmed medium or small shrubs
⬚   Max. height: 1–2m (3–6ft)
♦   Evergreen or deciduous
✳   Sun or part shade

Daphnes do not like being cut into old wood, although cuts made into one- or two-year-old wood will usually sprout away. Old specimens are best cleared of competing or smothering vegetation and left as they are. Time and light will do all the possible repairs. They are easy to raise from seed, and so new stock should be raised to replace spoiled specimens. Some species, like *D. laureola* will flower in deep shade, but others like *D. mezereum* and *D. tangutica* need full light.

Davidia   Cornaceae
Handkerchief tree

§   Single-stemmed tree
⬚   Max. height: 12m (40ft)
♦   Deciduous
✳   Sun or part shade

Davidia involucrata, the handkerchief tree, is not particularly competitive. In old gardens it is one of those species which gets suppressed by other more vigorous trees. Readmission of light will be the greatest ben-

Davidia involucrata

efit it can receive during rejuvenation. Removal of nearby competitors should also relieve root competition leading to drought, another of its dislikes. For the same reasons it is a good idea not to install any hard-working herbaceous gardening under a davidia; it should be treated like a magnolia in this respect.

Decaisnea   Lardizabalaceae
Decaisnea

§   Multi-stemmed large shrub
⬚   Max. height: 4–5m (13–16ft)
♦   Deciduous
✳   Sun or part shade

Decaisnea fargesii is grown for its metallic turquoise-blue bean-like pods. Old shrubs in too much shade will arch outwards and carry a great deal of dead wood. Pruning to ground level is not successful, but the arching process itself usually encourages the production of new shoots from low in the centre of the shrub. Prune out some old wood in spring to allow these new low shoots to grow unhindered. They will eventually replace all the older branches. Vigorous new shoots will take a few years to settle down to flowering. Decaisnea stems are soft and pithy inside.

Desfontainea   Loganiaceae
Desfontainea

§   Single-stemmed shrub
⬚   Max. height: 2m (6–10ft)
♦   Evergreen
✳   Sun or part shade

Once seen never forgotten, desfontainea is like a holly with red tubular flowers. It is not especially hardy. Old specimens do not respond well to cuts made into old branches and trunks. It is better to reshape the shrub by gentle pruning back in late spring of the younger healthy branches, and the removal if necessary of dead or misplaced branches.

Deutzia   Hydrangeaceae
Deutzia

§   Multi-stemmed medium to large shrub
⬚   Max. height: 2–3m (6–10ft)
♦   Deciduous
✳   Sun or light shade

Deutzias, like the related philadelphus, continuously throw up new stems from near the base, and these replace the older stems when they die, usually after five to six years.

Deutzia

Consequently this long-lived shrub is often found full of dead wood, and starved. A major thinning is required first, to see how much wood is dead, and how much alive. Take out all the dead material in early spring, and thin the live stems by 50 percent, to allow light into the bush and encourage the production of new stems from below. Taking the top out of remaining stems will encourage bushiness at the top, which in turn will take the light from the centre of the bush.

It is possible to cut deutzias right down and regrow all the stems, but they tend to be weak and whippy from this technique. It is better not to encourage such rapid growth.

Diervilla   Caprifoliaceae
Treat as for **Deutzia** (above)

Dipelta   Caprifoliaceae
Treat as for **Deutzia** (above)

Disanthus   Hamamelidaceae
Treat as for **Hamamelis** (page 114)

Elaeagnus pungens 'Maculata' showing reversion

Elaeagnus   Eleagnaceae

Elaeagnus

§ Single-stemmed or suckering shrubs
[] Max. height: 3–4m (10–13ft)
♦ Evergreen or deciduous
✼ Full sun or part shade

The common evergreen species, *Elaeagnus pungens*, is usually seen in its many variegated forms which need full sun. Hard pruning leads to die-back, and new shoots are only uncertainly produced and at odd angles. Better to shorten back and reshape the bush by cutting only into younger wood, in late spring. The shape is never elegant or even interesting, but with care it need not be gaunt. Watch for branches reverting to plain green, and cut them out.

The hybrid silvery-leaved evergreen *Elaeagnus* x *ebbingei* will tolerate a good deal of shade, especially as silver-leaved plants usually require sun. Prune as for *E. pungens*.

Elaeagnus commutata and *angustifolia* are deciduous suckering shrubs with silvery leaves. Both sucker from distant roots, and hard pruning of the main bush will encourage a strong crop of suckers. The stems grow fast, with a distinct leader, and have more poise than *Elaeagnus pungens*.

Embothrium

Chilean fire bush   Proteaceae

§ Narrow tree or large shrub
[] Max. height: 6–12m (20–40ft)
♦ Evergreen
✼ Dappled shade

Best planted in moist woodland glades, this plant's usual enemies are too much shade and hot dry roots. Specimens which have been shaded out at the bottom and have lost their lower branches cannot be persuaded to reclothe at low level by the readmission of light. Cutting off at ground level is not successful. Either live with a gaunt tree which flowers at the top, or replace it.

Embothrium coccineum 'Norquinco'

Enkianthus   Ericaceae

Enkianthus

§ Single- or multi-stemmed large shrub
[] Max. height: 4–5m (13–16ft)
♦ Deciduous
✼ Dappled shade

Beautiful small trees in the heather family, they have the typical root system of the Ericaceae, fibrous at the edges with few main woody roots. In old age they can become top-heavy and heave over. Be careful when clearing around overgrown specimens that new exposure does not topple them. Some thinning of the branches to relieve weight may be beneficial. Hard cutting back into large limbs is not successful.

Erica

See **Heaths and Heathers** (page 139)

Escallonia   Escalloniaceae

Escallonia

§ Single-stemmed medium or large shrubs
[] Max. height: 3m (10ft)
♦ Evergreen
✼ Full sun

Escallonias are easily killed by shade and hard pruning, even to ground level, is successful but only worthwhile if full light is readmitted. Moderate pruning to reshape can be carried out in late summer, but hard pruning is better done in spring. Old escallonia hedges may successfully be cut to ground level for vigorous regrowth. Heavy feeding and mulching works wonders.

Eucalyptus   Myrtaceae

Gum tree

§ Single-stemmed trees
[] Max. height: 20–30m (65–100ft)
♦ Evergreen
✼ Full sun

Eucalyptus only require good light to thrive, and if they have been grown that way require little attention. Winter-torn branches can be cut back in spring. Specimens which have been narrowed by shade will not fill out again at low level, but should go on to make good above, provided the root itself is secure. It is helpful to reintroduce them to full exposure gradually, to avoid heave. Younger specimens with trunks under 15cm (6in) diameter will readily sprout again from ground level, if cut down in spring. The root system is shallow and very hungry. It is difficult gardening underneath.

Eucalyptus aggregata

Eucryphia   Eucryphiaceae
Eucryphia

§ Large single-stemmed shrubs or small trees
[] Max. height: 10–12m (30–40ft)
♦ Evergreen or deciduous
✳ Sun or dappled shade

A small group of white summer-flowering trees. In neglected gardens their greatest enemy is shade, and drought brought about by the competition of other trees. If a eucryphia makes a large size and a dense canopy, that usually means it is happy. Drought and shade produce thin, leggy specimens. To rejuvenate, first readmit the light and remove root competition, then prune out wayward branches to reshape. Bald areas are difficult to reclothe. A replacement plant will be fast to grow and more successful in the long term than the uncertainty of cutting one off at ground level.

The deciduous *Eucryphia glutinosa* is the hardiest, and in old age can make a more round-headed small tree, rather than the tall evergreen column associated with *Eucryphia* x *nymansensis*.

Euonymus   Celastraceae
Spindle

§ Small to large bushy shrubs
[] Max. height: 2–3m (6–10ft)
♦ Deciduous or evergreen
✳ Sun or shade

The common spindle, *Euonymus europaeus*, can in winter be cut down low in youth or

Euonymus fortunei 'Emerald 'n' Gold'

middle age to regrow, but old specimens are better replaced. Flowering will stop for a few years after cutting low.

The evergreen *Euonymus japonicus* is one of the toughest of evergreens and can be seen lingering in heavy shade in old Victorian town gardens, or out in the blasting sun of Mediterranean gardens, where it is used like box to make low hedges. Cut it as hard as you like, in mid spring before bud-break.

The low bushy forms of *Euonymus fortunei*, like 'Emerald Gaiety' and 'Emerald 'n' Gold', are foliage evergreens which must have good light to stay dense and colourful. Readmit light first, and cut either hard or gently in spring, depending on the degree of disfigurement.

Exochorda   Rosaceae
Exochorda

§ Medium to large arching shrub
[] Max. height: 4m (13ft)
♦ Deciduous
✳ Sun or part shade

It is the habit of exochorda for old branches to arch over and new ones slowly to arise from the centre of the bush. Too much shade frequently prevents the younger shoots from developing properly. So the first remedy is to readmit light above, remove weed growth from below and give the shrub a year or two to show willing. Hard pruning of older limbs usually leads to die-back, but it is possible to take some of the stems right out at ground level to make space and light for new ones. Exochorda can live for 100 years or more.

Fagus sylvatica

Fagus   Fagaceae
Beech

§ Single-stemmed trees
[] Max. height: 30m (100ft)
♦ Deciduous
✳ Sun or part shade

The common beech, *Fagus sylvatica,* is massive in stature yet delicate in its tracery of twigs. It is shallow-rooted and difficult to garden below. Large wounds should be avoided. Branches which have been shortened back do not put out new shoots. Branches which must be removed in winter are better taken right out back to the trunk.

See also **Hedges** (pages 140–143)

Fallopia   Polygonaceae
Russian vine, mile-a-minute

§ Single- or multi-stemmed climber
[] Max. height: 25m (80ft)
♦ Deciduous
✳ Sun or part shade

The Russian vine *Fallopia baldschuanica* is a rampant climber, often used for the covering up of unsightly sheds and buildings. It can also be used for covering up gardens, and in neglected gardens it is often found playing the role of roof. Chop it down whenever is most convenient. Winter is kinder to the plant (if that is your intention), and the resulting mass of Brobdingnagian spaghetti is easier to dispose of in its leafless winter state. In summer after rain it is a nightmare to burn.

New shoots will spring up from the base and nearby, and mechanical and chemical controls may be necessary to confine it to barracks. Spraying in late summer is more effective than in spring.

Fatsia japonica

Fatsia Araliaceae
Fatsia

§ Multi-stemmed large shrub
☐ Max. height: 3m (10ft)
♦ Evergreen
✻ Shade or part shade

The glossy leaves of the plant sometimes erroneously called the castor oil plant make a good display indoors or in sheltered or seaside gardens. Old plants usually have many stems coming from the leafless base and a large overhanging head. The whole plant can be cut down in spring to just a few centimetres, but it is kinder to the plant to do it over two to three years, removing first those stems at the front which hang out the most, and thus readmitting light to the subsequent new shoots at the base. Potted plants respond less well to hard pruning.

Ficus Moraceae
Fig

§ Single- or multi-stemmed shrub or small tree
☐ Max. height: 9m (27ft)
♦ Deciduous
✻ Full sun

Figs (*Ficus carica*) are capable of making free-standing trees with heavy trunks which in old age may tear or break at the base, and this results in more new stems coming from the base of the plant. Plants to which this has happened will often carry a good deal of decay in the base of the plant, but are nevertheless capable of making good new growth for decades to come. Trunks of almost any age can be cut near to ground level in spring. The new shoots will be very soft and fast, and may need winter protection to get them through their first two to three winters.

There is no need to cut down old trunks, although if they look likely to break or topple, some reduction of weight can be beneficial.

Where a wall-trained fig has been allowed to run amok, it will take several years to get it back under control against the wall, and fruiting again. This is partly due to the retraining of the new growth, but also because the sudden vigour after heavy cutting takes time to settle down again.

Forsythia Oleaceae
Forsythia

§ Multi-stemmed medium or large shrubs
☐ Max. height: 3–4m (10–12ft)
♦ Deciduous
✻ Sun or part shade

Overgrown forsythias can be cut as hard as you like, in late winter. The stiffer, more upright varieties of *Forsythia* x *intermedia* respond better to being cut off at ground level. Flowering will recommence the next year. The wispier, pendulous *F. suspensa* is better thinned and shortened, and the strength of the existing stems retained. If cut very hard it can produce soft thin growth incapable of standing up.

Fothergilla Hamamelidaceae
Fothergilla

§ Multi-stemmed medium shrubs
☐ Max. height: 3m (10ft)
♦ Deciduous
✻ Sun or part shade

In shade fothergillas will become leggy and bare at the base. Readmission of light will encourage new shoots from low down. It is better to shorten the existing stems down to some lower shoots than to cut them off at

Fothergilla major in autumn

ground level. In shade the spectacular autumn colours are much less pronounced, and tufty white flowers very few.

Fraxinus Oleaceae
Ash

§ Single-stemmed tree
☐ Max. height: 20m (65ft)
♦ Deciduous
✻ Sun

Ash (*Fraxinus excelsior*) can become a weed species in many gardens. It is also very responsive to heavy pruning, like many another member of the olive family. So if a garden has many seedlings to be removed, remember that temporarily one might be saved and hard pruned in winter, as short-term screening. The manna ash, *Fraxinus ornus*, needs plenty of light to flower, and should be relieved of shade accordingly if it is to give its best.

Fremontodendron californicum

Fremontodendron Sterculiaceae
Fremontodendron

§ Slender single-stemmed shrub
☐ Max. height: 5–6m (6–10ft) on a wall
♦ Evergreen
✻ Full sun

Fremontodendrons are easy-come easy-go plants, with an unpredictable and sometimes short life span. Old specimens (10 years) do not enjoy hard pruning and are better replaced with a new plant. Specimens which are merely a little thin can be lightly pruned back in late spring, always to a live shoot. Gloves and a mask are recommended when handling fremontodendrons; their stems are covered with minute hairs which are highly irritant.

Fuchsia magellanica

Fuchsia   Onagraceae
Fuchsia

§ Medium or large shrubs
⟦⟧ Max. height: 2–3m (6–10ft)
♦ Deciduous
✳ Sun or part shade

The hardy fuchsias such as *F. magellanica* and its hybrids will often, after mild winters or in favoured gardens, carry a considerable amount of wood into the next season. They will also self-seed throughout Britain. Cold winters can cut them to the ground. So while it may be fun, and interesting to preserve the old wood of fuchsias, for their coppery peeling bark, do not count on those stems remaining for ever. Old trunks can be happily cut off at ground level to regrow. They are hungry plants, and appreciate renewed feeding and watering to revive them. In gardens where frosts are rare, *Fuchsia magellanica* can become almost a small tree.

Garrya   Garryaceae
Garrya

§ Large single-stemmed shrub
⟦⟧ Max. height: 5m (16ft)
♦ Evergreen
✳ Part shade

Old garryas can carry trunks the thickness of your thigh. They are commonly grown on a wall, although they will do perfectly well as a free-standing shrub. If the branches have been killed back by shade, or broken under the weight of age, garrya can be cut back to ground level in late winter and regrown as a bush, or retrained on a wall. Regrowth is fast, but the long tassel flowers will take three to four years to reappear.

Gaultheria   Ericaceae
Gaultheria

§ Suckering medium shrubs
⟦⟧ Max. height: 1–1.5m (3–5ft)
♦ Evergreen
✳ Shade or part sun

The common, vigorous *Gaultheria shallon* can be cut right down in spring and regrown. In dry shade the response is slower, and it may take two to three years to get back to 1.2m (4ft). Slower growing species are less willing to cooperate with hard pruning, and if the soil is not moist it may kill them.

Gaultheria mucronata (previously *Pernettya mucronata*) is grown for its brightly coloured berries in red, pink and white. It has few other virtues, other than being very hardy and capable of colonizing poor, dry or wet acid soils. Love it or hate it. In neglected gardens it can be found to have invaded far and wide with its fat underground stems, and

Garrya elliptica

then pushed up above to smother everything at ground level.

It is usually unisexual, so male and female plants are required for berries. If time and patience allow, identify which sex is which (assuming there are berries present) and then undertake some deep digging to get some of both sexes back within the required boundaries. Old stems may be cut down to resprout if required.

Genista   Leguminosae
Brooms and gorses

§ Single-stemmed wiry shrubs
⟦⟧ Max. height: 30cm–6m (1–20ft)
♦ Deciduous
✳ Full sun

Hard pruning is not successful on genistas. Spanish gorse, *Genista hispanica*, can become bald and leggy with age and shade, and is

Genista aetnensis

then better replaced. Dwarf and prostrate species infested with weed are also better replaced. The Mount Etna broom, *Genista aetnensis*, is a very tall, lax shrub, which may well rise 5–6m (16–20ft) above the neglected garden, and its airy habit should remain unimpaired by being smothered at ground level.

Ginkgo Ginkgoaceae

Maidenhair tree

§ Single-stemmed tree
[] Max. height: 20m (65ft)
♦ Deciduous
✳ Sun

Ginkgo biloba is a very long-lived tree, and asks no more than to be given plenty of light and hot summers. Its golden yellow autumn colour is without equal. Cold climates make for slow growth and frost damage to

Ginkgo biloba in autumn

unripened shoots. Frequently a double leader will develop following frost damage, and the best one only should be retained: cut out the runt in winter. Many of the selected forms of the tree are narrow ones suitable especially for use as street trees. Do not be surprised if even a seed-grown ginkgo remains quite narrow until it is 30–40 years old.

Griselinia Griseliniaceae

Griselinia

§ Single-stemmed shrub or small tree
[] Max. height: 6–7m (20–23ft)
♦ Evergreen
✳ Sun or part shade

A useful, crude evergreen with an elegant leaf, withstanding salt spray. Old plants may be cut down in spring to ground level to regrow, if generous light has been readmitted. Feed well. Plants which are simply too large and fat may be reshaped by pruning back the offending limbs in late spring.

Halesia Styracaceae

Halesia

§ Single-stemmed shrubs or trees
[] Max. height: 10m (30ft)
♦ Deciduous
✳ Sun or dappled shade

Old halesias do not respond well to hard pruning. Light should be readmitted, dead wood removed and some gentle removal of smaller branches undertaken to reshape the plant. Time must do the rest.

Hamamelis Hamamelidaceae

Witch hazel

§ Single-stemmed spreading shrubs
[] Max. height: 3m (10ft)
♦ Deciduous
✳ Sun or dappled shade

A witch hazel which is growing strongly can withstand a good deal of reshaping by the removal of branches up to 1cm ($^{1}/_{2}$in) thick. Always cut to a live shoot which will usually extend to replace the cut branch. Cut ends do not produce a crop of new soft shoots. More major cuts to witch hazel can lead to die-back, and should be avoided. Severely lopsided plants will not fill out again. The best treatment for an old witch hazel is often just to remove grass or herbaceous plants from over its root system, and mulch it with old compost or leaf mould, and to ensure it has sufficient light and moisture.

Halesia monticola var. vestita

Hebe Scrophulariaceae

Hebe

§ Single-stemmed bushy medium shrubs
[] Max. height: 2m (6ft)
♦ Evergreen
✳ Full sun

In neglected gardens the greatest enemy of hebes is lack of light. Shadow will make growth thin and flowerless, and a smothering of other plants will kill off affected branches. In both cases the best remedy is to readmit light and to cut the whole plant down to ground level in spring, and to feed well. Flowering will recommence in the second year.

Hamamelis mollis

Ivy slips in everywhere – even behind other climbers

Hedera
Araliaceae

Ivy

§ Single-stemmed climber or shrub
[] Max. height: 20m (65ft)
♦ Evergreen
❋ Sun or shade

Ivy (*Hedera helix*) loves an old garden. It would like it to itself. You will find it on the ground in shade, climbing up walls and trees, and wound deep into hedges. Most of the work required by ivy in old garden is removal, to put it within useful limits. In the right place, it is invaluable.

Consider first the two growth forms of ivy. In its climbing mode, it produces aerial roots, and clings to walls and trees until it reaches the top. Then its growth habit changes. It produces woodier stems with leaves all round the stem instead of on one side – the flowering growth. It is this part of the plant which, if propagated, produces the bush ivy, such an elegant evergreen shrub for shade.

Old trees can become absolutely clogged with ivy. Although it does not literally strangle the tree, it reduces its effective leaf canopy, weakening it, and provides the tree with a much increased wind resistance. Snow can sit on it by the ton. Bird-lime sits in it by the ton. Such trees benefit from having the volume of ivy drastically reduced, but there is no need to take it out altogether. If you try to take it all out the lazy way – by cutting through the main stem at the bottom, – it will reward you by dying and browning above but taking many years to rot and fall out of the tree, twig by miserable twig. It is far better to cut it out.

Ivy on walls can be more of a problem. The aerial roots can find their way into cracks, allowing water to penetrate and freeze, making the cracks wider still. On sound walls it is not a problem. On crumbly or poorly stuccoed walls it can be a serious problem. To remove it, simply cut it all off, then peel the stems away from the wall – a fiddly and difficult job. The wall will be marked underneath.

Golden-leaved ivies are always brightest in sun. Some, like 'Oro di Bogliasco' ('Goldheart') have a habit of producing very little cover low down on the wall, but fanning out higher up. To redress the balance, cut the lot down in winter, and pinch out the leaders as it comes back up over the next few years.

Where ivy on a wall is acceptable, but the canopy is too fat, it can be cut back hard to the wall in early spring every year. If there is mature growth at the top, it will soon rebuild itself if left alone for a year or two.

Ivy on the ground is perhaps the hardest to eradicate. The best method of attack is to spray in spring with glyphosate when the plant is in full leaf, using a detergent adjuvant in the mixture to make it stick to the shiny leaves. Six weeks later dig off and out all the ivy you can find. Then retreat the regrowth when it appears, for as often as is necessary.

Helichrysum
Compositae

Helichrysum

§ Single-stemmed bushy small shrubs
[] Max. height: 1m (3ft)
♦ Evergreen (silver)
❋ Full sun

The common hardy species, *Helichrysum italicum* (curry plant) and *Helichrysum splendidum*, can both be cut hard back in spring or even late summer after flowering to regrow. Older plants are less certain to respond and are better replaced from cuttings, since they are in any case not long lived.

Hibiscus
Malvaceae

Mallow

§ Single-stemmed twiggy shrubs
[] Max. height: 3m (10ft)
♦ Deciduous
❋ Full sun

Overgrown specimens of the hardy *Hibiscus syriacus* respond better to thinning and shortening of the branches to reshape them, rather than to being cut down low. Full light must be readmitted if flowering is to recommence or be generous.

Hibiscus syriacus 'Blue Bird'

Hippophae rhamnoides

Hippophae   Eleagnaceae
Sea buckthorn

§   Single-stemmed shrub or small tree
[]   Max. height: 4m (13ft)
♦   Deciduous
✱   Full sun

In old age sea buckthorn makes dense prickly trunks which do not respond to cutting low. If the top cannot be reshaped by judicious removal of a few major limbs in winter, then the plant is better replaced. Young wood can be pruned back, but the new shoots frequently come at awkward angles.

Hoheria   Malvaceae
Hoheria

§   Single-stemmed large shrub or small tree
[]   Max. height: 5–6m (16–20ft)
♦   Evergreen or deciduous
✱   Sun

Hoherias are not the hardiest of shrubs, and do well in the favoured climate of Cornwall and southern Ireland. All old specimens require is the readmission of adequate light all around, by pruning back neighbouring plants, and the removal of any lower branches which may have been killed by the plant's own shade. Hard pruning is better avoided, except to young fast-growing specimens.

Holodiscus   Rosaceae
Treat as for **Spiraea** (page 135)

Hydrangea   Hydrangeaceae
Hydrangea

§   Single- or multi-stemmed shrubs and climbers
[]   Max. height: 1–4m (3–12ft)
♦   Deciduous
✱   Sun or part shade

As a general rule, the more succulent the shoots of a hydrangea, the more it will respond well to hard pruning. Those with shaggy coppery bark are the least easy to prune hard.

Hortensias and lacecaps, (H. serrata)
Even huge old hydrangeas can still be cut off close to the ground in early spring with good results. Strong new shoots will come from ground level, and these may need thinning to keep a sensible number of the strongest, evenly spaced ones. Flowering will recommence in one or two years. As important as the pruning is generous feeding and watering.

HH. paniculata, quercifolia, sargentiana, aspera, heteromalla
More caution is needed with these species. Chopping down old single-trunked specimens frequently produces no response at all, and it is better to thin and reshape the plant in spring. Try to admit light to the base of the plant, so that new low shoots will develop properly. Old plants of *H. paniculata*, which require hard pruning every spring, are often best started again from cuttings and planted into new rich soil.

HH petiolaris, seemannii, etc
These are the climbing species. Heavy, voluminous specimens hanging out from walls can be cut in early spring, right back to the trunks themselves which cling to the wall with aerial roots. A new face will develop shortly. Where one has climbed into small trees or evergreens, some thinning out may be necessary to relieve the tree. Where it has climbed into larger trees – well, you should be so lucky!

Climbing hydrangeas will frequently spread along the ground, branching upwards to make a roving shrub. It is a fine sight, Keep it if you can.

Hypericum   Guttiferae
Rose of Sharon

§   Multi-stemmed small or medium shrubs
[]   Max. height: 1.5m (5ft)
♦   Semi-evergreen
✱   Sun or part shade

Old hypericums can be cut down hard in spring, and should be generously fed to encourage them. The rootstock of *Hypericum* 'Hidcote' can often be dug up and pulled apart into several new plants, throwing away the centre as you might with a herbaceous plant, and putting the offsets into newly enriched soil.

The low suckering *Hypericum calycinum* is often found to be riddled with weeds, and to facilitate the touch-weeding of invaders with glyphosate, it can be cut down to ground level and fed and mulched.

Hydrangea aspera (left); *Hydrangea paniculata* 'Floribunda' (right)

Ilex   Aquifoliaceae
Holly

§ Single- or multi-stemmed trees and shrubs
☐ Max. height: 6–20m (20–65ft)
♦ Evergreen
❋ Sun or part shade

Common holly (*Ilex aquifolium*) and its commoner hybrids (*Ilex* x *altaclarensis*, etc) will withstand heavy pruning in early spring and sprout again. However regrowth from large wounds is angular and haphazard, and may need attention over several subsequent years to thin it, so that the tree reshapes satisfactorily. Overall clipping, on the other hand, is an excellent option for heavily pruned hollies.

In the case of old or senescent trees which need major pruning, it is much more successful to cut them down to ground level – even trunks of 30–50cm (12–20in) across – than it is to cut the trunk down to waist or shoulder height. Regrowth is often astonishingly fast, and 1–2m (3–6ft) of good bushy growth can be expected in two years. Thin the new stems if you prefer.

Remember to sex the holly before you cut down, as it may be several years before flowering again. If it is the only male nearby, you will

Ilex aquifolium 'Aurea Marginata'

Itea ilicifolia

of course then have no berries on other female trees until flowering recommences.

Old hollies which are thin due to heavy shade will, given new light, fill out again over a few years. Watch for instability in hollies which have previously been heavily sheltered and drawn up by other trees. If necessary, prune the tree in early spring to prevent it heaving over.

See also **Hedges** (pages 140–143)

Itea   Escalloniaceae
Itea

§ Single-stemmed shrub
☐ Max. height: 3m (10ft)
♦ Evergreen
❋ Sun or part shade

Old plants of *Itea ilicifolia* which will not flower may often simply need more light and moisture to flourish. Cutting down old plants is not generally successful, and reshaping by shortening back to strong growth is a better plan.

Jasminum   Oleaceae
Jasmine

§ Single- or multi-stemmed shrubs and climbers
☐ Max. height: 3–4m (10–12ft)
♦ Mostly deciduous
❋ Mostly sun

Winter jasmine (*Jasminum nudiflorum*) is a lax easy come easy go shrub which can be treated with considerable disrespect. Rampant old plants are frequently overwhelmed by surrounding layers, made where stems have touched the ground. Plants of a medium age may have older wood thinned out and new wood vigorously shortened back. Very old plants are better replaced by a layer. This species will flower in a surprising degree of shade.

Shrubby *Jasminum revolutum* cannot be given the same hard treatment. Plants of a moderate age, where the bark is still green, will shoot well from hard cutting, but older scaly bark is less willing to shoot out. Regrowth is often awkward and angular.

Old plants of summer jasmine (*Jasminum officinale*) can make vast dreary tangles of dead stems, like monstrous birds' nests. In spring tease out as best you can a living stem which begins reasonably low on the plant, and chop away above it all the old tangle. The remaining stem can be shortened back to good low buds and the plant fed and mulched. New lower shoots may appear, but it is safer and faster to keep one old stem. Flowering and perfume will take two to three years to re-establish.

Jasminum officinale

Juglans   Juglandaceae
Walnut

§ Single-stemmed tree
☐ Max. height: 20m (65ft)
♦ Deciduous
✳ Sun

Walnuts are great self-seeders; buried in odd corners by squirrels, they shoot up into sizeable trees before you know it. They can be pruned, but taking out whole branches in winter is better than shortening them back. The sap rises early, so beware of cutting in a mild spell in early spring, in case the wound bleeds badly. The wood can be very valuable.

Juniperus   Cupressaceae
Juniper

§ Single- or multi-stemmed shrub/small trees
☐ Max. height: 6m (20ft)
♦ Evergreen
✳ Full sun

The common juniper, *Juniperus communis*, has an enormously wide distribution in the northern hemisphere. Its habit varies from tall and upright, through rounded, to the prostrate. It can live to a great age, but usually passes way beyond the garden-worthy long before it gets old. Shabby plants, especially of the upright 'Hibernica', should be replaced.

The best known of the low-growing junipers are *Juniperus sabina* 'Tamariscifolia' and *J.* x *media* 'Pfitzeriana'. Both seem so slow in their early years, and then suddenly they are yards across, spreading out over paths in all directions and doubling like dough. Every bit of pruning seems to show most cruelly.

'Tamariscifolia' and the other junipers whose low branches point downwards are best pruned by cutting them back 'invisibly', underneath the canopy. Cut in spring branches up to 6–7cm (2½–3in) in diameter. The less you cut the better. Thinning out the 'fringe' around its edges may help to disguise the deed.

Junipers with arching branches that weep at the tip, like 'Pfitzeriana', are even harder to cut satisfactorily. Cutting back trunks 10–15cm (4–6in) across in spring frequently produces no new shoots at all, or the diverted strength will go into some backwards-pointing side branch, which tries to cross back into the middle of the plant, leaving the stump still bare and a great hole in the bush. The best answer with these junipers is to nibble them all over, pruning lightly, to halt if not reduce the spread. If a major reduction is needed, then you must replant.

Kalmia   Ericaceae
Mountain laurel, calico bush

§ Single-stemmed or suckering shrubs
☐ Max. height: 3–4m (10–12ft)
♦ Evergreen
✳ Full sun

Kalmias are undemanding plants so long as they have plenty of light, a genuinely moist soil, and above all an acid soil. Solve these problems first. Shade and root competition from large trees, causing dryness, are often the principal problems.

Kalmia latifolia

Large and leggy plants of *Kalmia latifolia* are best shortened gradually over a few years, cutting back always to live shoots, and encouraging low branches to fill out the base of the plant once more.

The smaller, suckering *Kalmia angustifolia* has the same growing requirements, which need to be met for successful rejuvenation. At best cut out the oldest bowed stems and allow new shoots to fill the space. At worst, dig up a clump of younger suckers, dig out all the rest of the old plant, dig over and replenish the soil, and replant the suckers.

Kerria   Rosaceae
Jew's mallow

§ Suckering shrub
☐ Max. height: 2–3m (6–10ft)
♦ Deciduous
✳ Sun or part shade

Kerria is a tough, easy plant. Old colonies should be pruned in early summer after flow-

ering. Cut out old bowed stems, leaving evenly spaced strong stems. Feed and mulch the clump well. If the clump has spread too far, chop it back with a spade to the desired limits. Very old clumps in tired dry, soil may be lifted in winter, the soil replenished, and a few younger portions only of the clump replanted.

Kolkwitzia   Caprifoliaceae
Beauty bush

§ Single- or multi-stemmed shrub
☐ Max. height: 3m (10ft)
♦ Deciduous
✳ Sun or dappled shade

It is tempting to treat *Kolkwitzia amabilis* like a philadelphus, as the habit is similar. It flowers on old stems and makes a large vase-shaped bush, arching over with age.

But it is less willing to regenerate from cutting down low. If there are plenty of young shoots coming from low down, then older stems may be removed in early spring. But If there appears only to be really one large woody trunk, then it is better to thin out the canopy, and reduce the overhang, reshaping it over two to three years.

Kolkwitzia amabilis

Laburnum x *watereri*

Laburnum   Leguminosae
Golden Rain

§ Single-stemmed trees
❑ Max. height: 7m (22ft)
♦ Deciduous
✳ Sun

On shallow soils, old laburnums are prone to fall over. This applies to transplanted specimen trees more than self-sown trees. That said, falling over does not always kill them, and they can soldier on for decades on one elbow, so long as no one gardens them to death and forces them back on to their feet. In nature at least, there is no hurry for hospital beds.

As members of the pea family, laburnums do not take kindly to cuts made across major limbs, and will not sprout out usefully. However, a high cut often induces a shoot to appear low down out of surprisingly old wood, and these can be grown on to make new major limbs.

Laburnums used formally on pergolas and other structures and allowed to go rank can usually have their unwanted new limbs cut off back to the trunk, and new shoots tied in and developed.

Larix (Larch)   Pinaceae
Treat as for **Picea** (page 125)

Laurus   Lauraceae
Bay

§ Single- or multi-stemmed trees
❑ Max. height: 6m (20ft)
♦ Evergreen
✳ Sun

Bay (*Laurus nobilis*) in an ideal climate makes a clean-stemmed tree. In cool temperate gardens it is more often seen as a multi-stemmed large shrub or tree. Severe winters can cut it to the ground, and it will spring up again afterwards. It can also be cut to the ground in spring if old trunks show signs of die-back. However, when decay begins to get into the base of the tree, the new stems are rarely strong or healthy enough to make a good new plant, and the thing is better replaced.

Lavandula   Labiatae
Lavender

§ Single- or multi-stemmed shrub
❑ Max. height: 1m (3ft)
♦ Evergreen
✳ Full sun

Depending upon the soil and the variety, and provided they have not been overtaken by shade, lavenders may live to 15 or 20 years. Unless conditions are going to be sufficiently sunny again there is little point preserving lavenders. They resent cuts into old wood and do not sprout successfully. They are reluctant to fill holes in the canopy, even when light is readmitted. Nor do they transplant well. But in a sunny place, old gaunt lavenders can have a certain charm, and by the removal of the more wayward outgrowths in late spring, they can be retained as a rather craggy bush by regular seasonal pruning at the edges.

Lavatera   Malvaceae
Shrubby mallow

§ Single- or multi-stemmed shrub
❑ Max. height: 4m (13ft)
♦ Semi-evergreen
✳ Full sun

Lavatera is a relatively short lived shrub, and five to eight years is a long life. They grow fast and provide generous short term colour, but beware of them smothering more important plants and evergreens. Healthy old lavateras can be cut down low in late spring and will soon be flowering again. (It is important to prune them every year, especially on rich soils where the growth can be lush and weak.) But when the plant has reached three- or four-years old it is time to be thinking about taking a cutting for replacement.

Laurus nobilis 'Aurea'

Leycesteria   Caprifoliaceae

Pheasant berry

§   Multi-stemmed shrub
▯   Max. height: 3–4m (10–12ft)
♦   Semi-evergreen
✳   Sun or shade

Leycesteria formosa is a prolific self-seeder, and will spread itself around a garden very easily, finding its way in amongst other shrubs, cracks in paths and paving, and even into wall tops. Its greatest attraction is the bloom on its grey-green young stems. The drooping flowers and clusters of berries are good, but the berries can be messy underfoot and they smell unpleasant. Plants which have achieved 3m (10ft) or more may well be too woody at the base to regenerate well from cutting down low, but there is no virtue in not trying. Younger plants can be happily cut down to a few centimetres in early spring, producing a fountain of 1–2m (3–6ft) shoots during the first season. Flowering is better in sun. The plant is generally tidier and better behaved on under-fed soils.

Ligustrum   Oleaceae

Privet

§   Single- or multi-stemmed trees or shrubs
▯   Max. height: 5–10m (15–30ft)
♦   Evergreen and deciduous
✳   Sun or part shade.

All privets respond well to hard pruning in late winter. Fine tree-like species with good flowers such as *Ligustrum lucidum* are better reshaped as trees, taking out misplaced branches to balance the canopy. If necessary they can be cut down low and will make a spectacularly fast multi-stemmed small tree.

Rank specimens of the hedging privet, *Ligustrum ovalifolium* and its golden form 'Aureum', can both be cut down low, and will very quickly regrow to a more controllable size.

Privets will tolerate poor conditions, but nevertheless they are hungry plants: to produce good regeneration feeding is helpful.

See also **Hedges** (pages 140–143)

Liquidambar (Sweet gum)

Hamamelidaceae
Treat as for **Fagus** (page 111)

Liriodendron (Tulip tree)

Magnoliaceae
Treat as for **Fagus** (page 111)

Lonicera perclymenum

Lonicera   Caprifoliaceae

Honeysuckle

§   Single- or multi-stemmed shrubs and climbers
▯   Max. height: 3–4m (10–12ft)
♦   Deciduous and evergreen
✳   Sun or dappled shade

The shrubby honeysuckles will all stand being cut down low if they have become massively top-heavy. More often than not there are low stems which can be retained when the main stems are cut out.

Lupinus arboreus

Flowering species like *L. fragrantissima* are better thinned and reshaped as flowering is better on old wood.

The hedging species *L. nitida* and 'ground cover' species can both be cut off at the base and will very quickly refurnish.

The climbing honeysuckles (*Lonicera japonica, periclymenum, sempervirens, × tellmanniana* etc) also sprout well after being cut hard in early spring, but it is safer to cut them back to about 2m (6ft) rather than lower down. This means there are more dormant buds left to sprout, and it also retains the plant's foothold on its support, which saves doing all that initial training again. Feed and water well.

Lupinus   Leguminosae

Tree lupin

§   Single-stemmed bushy shrub
▯   Max. height: 2m (6ft)
♦   Evergreen
✳   Full sun

Tree lupins, *Lupinus arboreus*, require full sun to thrive. They do not respond to hard pruning. They are short-lived plants and better replaced with seedlings when they begin to get old. However, misplaced branches can be tidied back to the canopy, and a more regular shape achieved. But do not expect regrowth from the cuts. Seedlings are easily raised and may occur naturally. Most purchased plants are a strong acid yellow. If you have a paler form and prefer it, keep it going by seedlings, which mostly come true.

Magnolia x *soulangeana* 'Lennei Alba'

A magnolia seed pod ripens and opens

Magnolia   Magnoliaceae

Magnolia

§ Single- or multi-stemmed trees or shrubs
☐ Max. height: 3–20m (10–65ft)
♦ Evergreen and deciduous
✻ Sun

Magnolias are not easy to prune: they are not cooperative. But they are not as unresponsive as some people believe.

Old specimens which have become leggy at the base cannot be refurnished at that level except through time and the dropping of the lowest existing branches. Remember, many magnolias are really small or even large trees: it is sometimes better when a plant has lost lower branches to take off a few more and turn it into a proper tree.

Magnolias withstand pruning best when the cuts are made into strongly growing wood. This means that it is possible to take a 10cm (4in) diameter branch off the trunk of a healthy vigorous *Magnolia kobus* in mid spring, and it will callus over and heal with no ill effect. It is possible to cut back into 1–3cm ($^1/_2$–1 $^1/_2$in) thick wood at any time. The cuts will not sprout, but the next shoot behind will take over and develop in its place.

But it is not possible to cut back hard a low, shaded branch into wood 5–10cm (2–4in) thick and expect new shoots to come forward and cover the space. Such cuts may produce no response at all, or may even begin to die back. A shaded branch is always less responsive than one higher on the shrub and actively growing upwards.

Nor is it a good idea ever to cut the top out of a magnolia. A major wound at the top of the central trunk spells the beginning of the end. You can of course take the top out of a very young magnolia, into merely twiggy growth, and it will then quickly be replaced by another, so long as it is already growing hard.

The magnolias which are hard to prune are those which are growing poorly, because they are either senile, or stressed through drought, hunger, or successive seasons of frost damage. Plants such as these are best left alone until you can get them into better health. Then you can begin gently to reshape them. Very old trees and shrubs are best simply left to their own devices, perhaps with the removal of significant dead wood to reduce the weight.

Mahonia   Berberidaceae

Mahonia

§ Multi-stemmed or suckering shrubs
☐ Max. height: 2–4m (6–12ft)
♦ Evergreen
✻ Sun or shade

Mahonia japonica, lomariifolia, 'Charity' etc are all fat-stemmed winter-flowering evergreens which will withstand heavy pruning remarkably well. It is, however, better to do it gradually, cutting down long gangly stems at two to three per year in spring, until the bush is refurnished. The shock of cutting down all the stems at once severely shocks the plant, and regrowth is correspondingly weaker.

These mahonias will thrive in quite deep shade, but they flower better and are denser in sun. Large specimens do not move well.

The suckering *Mahonia aquifolium* is a great survivor often found in old gardens. This species and its hybrids will also respond to pruning, by taking out some of the older stems which have become bare at the base. Again, do it gradually for best results. You will never kill this plant, but can slow it down enormously by overzealous pruning.

Mahonias are susceptible to a severely debilitating fungal rust. Specimens weak with rust damage (mottled orangey leaves and some defoliation) are better treated first or concurrently for rust, to improve the chances of successful pruning.

Mahonia japonica

Malus floribunda

Malus   Rosaceae
Apple

§ **Single-stemmed trees**
☐ **Max. height: 8m (25ft)**
♦ **Deciduous**
✳ **Sun**

As well as the domestic apple, there are innumerable other good crabs and, of course, the species like *Malus floribunda*, *hupehensis*, *toringoides* and *transitoria*. As ornamentals all they require is good light. Heavy old trees may be given help by gently thinning away in winter some of the branches, to reduce the weight and let in light and air. But too heavy cutting will produce water shoots and make work in removing them again.

Neglected fruiting apples will require different treatments according to their form, to get them back into manageable order. The more restricted forms, like espaliers and fans, respond to the necessary heavy pruning by producing a lot of soft watershoots, which need a great deal of careful and patient pruning, summer and winter, to get them back into steadier fruiting growth. For serious fruit production it may be more efficient to start again with a new tree.

Free-standing trees can be easier to restore to size and order. There will be a need to lower the canopy, take out crossing major branches to let light in to ripen the fruit throughout, and to thin lightly the remaining branches. It is a good job for a crisp winter's day.

Metasequoia (Dawn redwood)
Taxodiaceae
Treat as for **Picea** (page 125)

Morus   Moraceae
Mulberry

§ **Single-stemmed tree**
☐ **Max. height: 7m (20ft)**
♦ **Deciduous**
✳ **Sun**

The mulberry, *Morus nigra*, will withstand heavy pruning very well. Old trees eventually become top-heavy, piling cloud upon cloud of dense branches, until often the whole thing keels over, either in a gale, or of its own accord.

Old mulberries have wonderful character, especially in the trunk and major branches. They can be saved from falling over by major pruning, shortening back the major limbs in winter by as much as 60 percent, and developing a new branch structure from this framework.

Alternatively, there may already be long watershoots arising from the centre of the tree, and these can be used to replace older branches, on a more gradual basis over several years.

Trees which have a severe lean may be propped and hard pruned to relieve the weight. They usually recover and make a picturesque specimen for many more years.

A storm-damaged mulberry at Great Dixter sprouts away after major cutting back.

Myrtus   Myrtaceae
Myrtle

§ **Multi-stemmed shrub or small tree**
☐ **Max. height: 4–5m (12–15ft)**
♦ **Evergreen**
✳ **Sun**

Myrtles are better suited to milder gardens. Severe winters will kill them to ground level but they usually sprout up again the next year. They can be similarly pruned in late winter if necessary. In climates where myrtles thrive, their bark in old age is one of their attractions, and a damaged canopy would be better tidied up by pruning, rather than lose all those years' thickening of the trunk or trunks by cutting them right down.

Nandina   Berberidaceae
Sacred Bamboo

§ **Multi-stemmed shrub**
☐ **Max. height: 2m (6ft)**
♦ **Deciduous**
✳ **Full sun**

A slow-growing shrub not unlike a fine *Mahonia japonica* in habit. In neglected gardens it tends to be simply overwhelmed by more vigorous species, and retains just a few wispy leaves at the top.

Once a stem has set off from the base of the plant it does not branch, and shortening it back will not produce new shoots at the top. Instead you must cut out old stems at the bottom and allow any new shoots at the base to replace them. In neglected and shaded plants there may, of course, be no new basal shoots present, in which case, having readmitted the light, then feed, mulch and water well, and expect in a year or two to see some new shoots to cut back to.

Neillia thibetica

Neillia   Rosaceae

Neillia

§ Multi-stemmed shrub
☐ Max. height: 3m (10ft)
♦ Deciduous
✳ Sun or dappled shade

Neillia is a tough, easy shrub, which may be treated as for philadelphus. It dislikes dry soils, so if root competition has become severe, give a good mulch regularly.

Nymphaea   Nymphaeaceae

Water-lily

§ Aquatic perennial
☐ Max. spread: 30m (100ft)
♦ Deciduous
✳ Sun

Strong varieties of water-lily can virtually take over even a large pond. Summer is the time to tackle them. Working in waders or from a boat, drag out by the boatload as much of the lily and its roots as you can get. Old colonies will almost certainly survive and spring up again in part after this treatment, but you may wish to replant some in a basket to be certain.

Olearia   Compositae

Daisy bush

§ Single- or multi-stemmed shrubs
☐ Max. height: 2–3m (6–10ft)
♦ Evergreen
✳ Full sun

Old but vigorous olearias can happily be cut down low in mid to late spring to regrow. They dislike shade, and can quickly become misshapen by the company of more vigorous neighbours. Very old plants of *Olearia macrodonta* may fail to respond, but the hardiest species, *Olearia* x *haastii*, will always rise again from the ground.

Osmanthus   Oleaceae

Osmanthus

§ Single-stemmed shrubs
☐ Max. height: 2–5m (6–15ft)
♦ Evergreen
✳ Sun

All osmanthus respond well to being pruned down low, but cut stumps high in the bush do not often sprout unless they are growing vigorously. However, misplaced branches can be cut back within the canopy, to a live bud, where they will fill out again. It is better to try reshaping before resorting to cutting down, if only to keep the perfumed flowers going (e.g. *Osmanthus* x *burkwoodii*, *decorus* and *delavayi*). Picking for indoors is the best way to keep wayward shoots in order.

Ozothamnus   Compositae

Ozothamnus

§ Single- or multi-stemmed shrubs
☐ Max. height: 2–3m (6–10ft)
♦ Evergreen
✳ Full sun

Like many another Australasian plant with narrow leaves, ozothamnus is naturally a plant for hot, open positions. It is easily spoiled by the shade of encroaching neighbours, especially in softer, moister climates, and is not easily persuaded to refurnish itself. Nor is it especially hardy. Old plants which have become leggy and straggly will occasionally sprout again from the base after pruning down in late spring, but they are rarely as good again. It is much better to start again with a young plant which can be pinched out while young and made to form a fuller bush.

Nymphaea 'Moorei'

Osmanthus x *burkwoodii*

Paeonia   Ranunculaceae

Tree peony

§ Multi-stemmed shrub
☐ Max. height: 2–3m (6–10ft)
♦ Deciduous
✳ Sun or part shade

The tree peonies most likely to survive in neglected gardens are *Paeonia delavayi* (crimson) and its varieties *ludlowii* and *lutea* (yellow). These self-seed freely, and such progeny may posses good or indifferent flowers. Vigorous old plants with good-sized flowers are worth keeping going by readmitting light, and pruning out low any broken or senescent stems. This will allow newer stems to take their place in full light. Very old plants with considerable decay in the central crown may be better scrapped and replaced. A generous feed and mulch is always beneficial.

The Moutan peony and its cultivars (*Paeonia suffruticosa* and cvs) is a less vigorous plant and much less of a survivor. Rangy old plants should be generously fed and watered, and brought back to good health if possible, before giving minimal pruning in spring, back to a well placed bud.

Parrotia persica in its typical dome shape

Parrotia   Hamamelidaceae

Ironwood Tree

§ Single-stemmed tree
▯ Max. height: 6m (20ft)
♦ Deciduous
❋ Sun

Most of the parrotias in cultivation form a dome-shaped tree broader than it is tall. A smothering of shrubs, brambles and long grass can shade out the fringe of the tree. But if it is cleared around, the lower branches will gradually lean down again and fill the space. Pruning is best kept to a minimum otherwise. It is not possible to undo this domed habit by pruning, although the dome can be put on a higher leg by doing so. Make sure the tree has plenty of light, or the little scarlet flowers will not be produced in spring.

Parthenocissus   Vitaceae

Virginia Creeper

§ Climbers
▯ Max. height: 30m (100ft)
♦ Deciduous
❋ Sun or shade

Virginia creeper, *Parthenocissus quinquefolia*, is a rampant climber known for its autumn colours. It clings by means of suckers on long tendrils. The smaller *Parthenocissus tricuspidata* clings by groups of suckers growing right from the stems. Both will easily cover houses and trees.

Both can be cut down low, but the response from old trunks 10–20cm (4–8in) across is unpredictable. (Stems 5–8cm (2–3in) across sprout much better.) It is better to keep the lowest live limb as the basis for new cover.

Neither of these climbers is destructive of stonework as is ivy, but they can build up a considerable weight on a wall, and they attract birds' nests and therefore many flies around windows.

Parthenocissus can be allowed to climb trees so long as they are not allowed to smother them. Conifers and evergreen are especially at risk. But then a streak or two of *Parthenocissus henryana*, in full autumn glory, through a blue spruce, is sheer magic.

Pernettya   Ericaceae
See under **Gaultheria** (page 113)

Parthenocissus offers a warm embrace

Philadelphus   Hydrangeaceae

Mock orange

§ Multi-stemmed shrub
▯ Max. height: 2–3m (6–10ft)
♦ Deciduous
❋ Sun

Who would be without the perfume of philadelphus in high summer? Plants will live for many decades, forever renewing the stems from the base, and withstanding a great deal of shade and overgrowth.

Where space allows, old plants of the plain old *Philadelphus coronarius* can be left alone unpruned to make a 3–4m (10–12ft) mound. In more constrained situations, any philadelphus can have its stems thinned out drastically at the base, and the same result will inevitably follow to the mushroom-head of the stems, as they lean over at the top. In a large specimen of *Philadelphus* 'Virginal' this is no easy task. It may seem easier to chop the whole lot off at ground level and start again. The plant will stand it, but it produces such a rush of soft stems, that it is better to thin the plant instead. No matter if you lose a lot of the mushroom-head in the disentangling process; it will soon regrow. Light will be readmitted to the centre, and the stems which remain will thrive, and new ones follow in due course. Prune in winter, to minimize damage to buds. So long as the plant is healthy, feeding is not necessary and indeed would make the new growth even softer.

Phillyrea latifolia

Phillyrea   Oleaceae

Phillyrea

§ Single-stemmed small shrubs or trees
[] Max. height: 10m (30ft)
♦ Evergreen
✱ Full sun

Lustrous dark evergreens good for clipping into shape or making a dense evergreen small tree. *Phillyrea latifolia* is often found in old gardens as a round-headed tree which can break under the weight of snow. When shaded by other trees it can become gaunt and tall. It will withstand heavy pruning in early spring, either of major limbs which shoot well, or down to the ground.

Phlomis   Labiatae

Jerusalem sage

§ Single- or multi-stemmed shrub
[] Max. height: 2m (6ft)
♦ Evergreen
✱ Full sun

Given warmth and good drainage, phlomis can survive over several decades. Its greatest enemy, like most grey-leaved plants, is shade. A lank specimen with a bare base can be encouraged to fill again at the base by careful pruning back to a bud in late spring of unwanted portions of the bush, until gradually, over two to three years, the canopy is shortened and filled out. Harder pruning is possible, taking it low down to the ground, but it is not always successful on very old plants. Gentle feeding in midsummer only is beneficial.

Photinia   Rosaceae

Photinia

§ Single-stemmed shrubs or small trees
[] Max. height: 4–8m (12–25ft)
♦ Mainly evergreen
✱ Sun

Photinia x *fraseri* and its varieties may be very glamorous when their new foliage is glowing scarlet, but the rest of the time they are relatively undistinguished plants. They do not have much poise. Pruning is best kept to a minimum,

Photinia davidiana (syn. *Stranvaesia davidiana*)

cutting out misplaced or bent branches, and making the best of the shape. Hard pruning to fill gaps is not usually successful. *Photinia davidiana* is the correct name for the large shrub known previously as *Stranvaesia davidiana*.

Phygelius   Scrophulariaceae

Cape figwort

§ Suckering shrub
[] Max. height: 2m (6ft)
♦ Semi-evergreen
✱ Sun

Phygelius capensis and *P. aequalis* are tough, easy plants. The first of these especially will survive in old gardens, not doing much, but not dying either.

Very old clumps in tired, dry soil may be lifted in winter, the soil replenished, and a few younger, outer portions only of the clump replanted. Having got it going again well in the right place, bits of the old plant will surface again. Weedkillers may be necessary to finish them off.

Younger colonies may be cut to ground level and heavily fed and mulched. They will flower again in the first year.

Physocarpus   Rosaceae

Nine bark

§ Multi-stemmed large shrub
[] Max. height: 3–4m (10–12ft)
♦ Deciduous
✱ Sun or part shade

Coarse deciduous shrubs, grown not for their flowers, but for the foliage of the golden forms. Treat as for **Philadelphus** (page 124).

Picea   Pinaceae

Spruce

§ Single-stemmed conifer
[] Max. height: 1–30m (3–100ft)
♦ Evergreen
✱ Sun

All the spruces, including the Christmas tree, *Picea abies*, the pendulous Serbian spruce, *Picea omorika*, and the blue *Picea pungens* 'Koster', only require good light and sufficient rainfall to thrive. These are frequently planted in hot dry gardens where, with severe root competition from other trees, the effective drought can make them sad-looking specimens. Removing root competition by taking out other close-by trees may improve matters, but not entirely. Do not feel obliged to save a tired-looking specimen in the hope of better things: they may never come.

The same requirement for coolness and moisture applies to dwarf forms like *Picea glauca* var. *albertiana* 'Conica' and *P. mariana* 'Nana'. In extreme heat and drought, severe leaf loss may be due to infestation with red spider mite, for which the best cure is regular dousing of the canopy with plain water.

Phygelius hybrid

Pieris 'Forest Flame' flowers and new foliage

Pieris   Ericaceae

Pieris

§
Single- or multi-stemmed shrubs
▯ Max. height: 3–10m (10–30ft)
♦ Evergreen
✽ Dappled shade

Although pieris can regrow from being cut down low, the larger species such as *P. formosa* and its varieties especially are better pruned back gradually, taking wayward branches back to a green shoot in the main framework, and allowing them to fill out. Otherwise the beauty of the peeling older bark is lost. If necessary, whole branches can be cut back hard in mid spring. Even quite sizeable stumps will sprout, although some die-back may follow.

Too much shade reduces flowering, and the readmission of sufficient light is important. *Pieris floribunda* is happiest of all in full sun, and can have clumps of its canopy thinned away, like florets from a cauliflower, to reduce the density if sheer weight or snow damage makes it necessary.

Pinus   Pinaceae

Pine

§
Single-stemmed conifer
▯ Max. height: 2–25m (6–80ft)
♦ Evergreen
✽ Sun

Pines only require good light to thrive, and will withstand considerable drought. In old age the crowns tend to be more spreading than in other forest conifers such as firs and spruces, and the better part of their character often only develops with age. The Scots pine especially, *Pinus sylvestris*, can make an elegant yet craggy old tree with surprisingly few large, high branches. Make use of this habit if you can.

Younger trees, which have been weakened by shade and overcrowding but have not lost their leaders, will go on to make acceptable but not fine trees in the long term, so long as they are still wind-firm under increased exposure.

Prune pines only as much as is really necessary, taking out dead or largely dead branches back right to the trunk in winter.

Species which are very fast- and soft-growing in garden conditions, such as the Bhutan pine, *Pinus wallichiana*, may be found to suffer badly from snow and gale damage. If the

From left to right:
Larix decidua in autumn
A grove of *Metasequoia glyptostroboides*
Pinus pinea, with typical flat crowns
Pinus sylvestris in old age

Piptanthus nepalensis

Piptanthus   Leguminosae

Evergreen laburnum

§   Multi-stemmed sometimes suckering shrub
▯   Max. height: 3–4m (10–12ft)
♦   Semi-evergreen
❋   Full sun

Shade is the biggest enemy of piptanthus in overgrown gardens. Prune back gently in spring, to live shoots only, until the balance is restored. Older plants may subsequently produce no new shoots low down, and will be better replaced. Their whole beauty is in their freshness. They are very fast to establish as seedlings.

Pittosporum   Pittosporaceae

Pittosporum

§   Single- stemmed shrubs or small trees
▯   Max. height: 5m (16ft)
♦   Evergreen
❋   Full sun

Salt-tolerant Australasian evergreens for milder gardens. The hardiest species is *Pittosporum tenuifolium*, which in its non-dwarf forms will make a small tree. Pruning into old wood is not successful, and if at all possible plants should be reshaped by cutting only recent wood in late spring. Parts of trees which have been shaded out by neighbouring plants are unlikely to refurnish themselves even when light is readmitted.

Platanus   Platanaceae

Plane

§   Single-stemmed trees
▯   Max. height: 25m (80ft)
♦   Deciduous
❋   Sun or part shade

Planes, and especially the London plane, *Platanus* x *hispanica*, are most tolerant of heavy pruning. Heavy crown thinning is most effective in reducing their heavy shade where necessary, cutting out whole branches in winter. You can, if absolutely necessary, shorten back all the branches of a plane once every few years, and treat it as a pollard tree. It is ugly but possible.

Populus   Salicaceae

Poplar

§   Single-stemmed tree
▯   Max. height: 25m (80ft)
♦   Deciduous
❋   Sun

Poplars are not the most garden-worthy of trees, so they are not often grown, although the ochres and oranges and yellows of the opening buds in spring can be a joy. Beware of felling a live healthy poplar as suckers can arise from the roots, vigorously and at a considerable distance from the tree. Chemical treatment will be necessary over several years to subdue them. Mechanical damage to

Populus x *candicans* 'Aurora'

Pollarding a plane tree

shallow roots from digging can also provoke suckering.

The white-variegated *Populus* x *candicans* 'Aurora' is a small tree which loses the brilliancy of its variegation when allowed to grow away freely. Hard pruning in late winter, back to a framework of branches, will provoke an explosion of colourful new growth the following year.

Potentilla   Rosaceae

Shrubby potentilla

§   Multi-stemmed shrubs
▯   Max. height: 1.5m (5ft)
♦   Deciduous
❋   Full sun

In old gardens shade, drought and hunger are the enemies of potentillas (*Potentilla fruticosa, dahurica, arbuscula* and cultivars). Give them light. Give them a moist soil which is not being sucked dry by tree roots. Give them a mulch of rich manure or fertilizer. Then if you cut them back hard in mid spring – as crudely as you like – they will shoot away like wild horses. Flowering will at once be free as ever.

An old flowering cherry, with *Prunus laurocerasus* flowers (inset)

Prunus

This genus contains many different groups each with its own set of requirements.

Almonds and plums: old congested plums, including the purple-leaved *Prunus cerasifera* 'Pissardii', should be pruned gently in late summer, taking out crossing branches and thinning the canopy if necessary. Heavy pruning will simply induce large numbers of long watershoots, compounding the problem of congestion and making more work.

Wild and flowering cherries: There are many kinds of attractively flowering cherry, from the vigorous, wild *Prunus avium* and *P. cerasus*, to the cultivated Japanese cherries with their elegant, spreading forms. Wild cherries withstand but do not enjoy heavy pruning in late summer. It is better to take out misplaced branches entirely than to shorten back.

Flowering cherries like 'Kanzan' and 'Shirofugen', the autumn-flowering *Prunus* x *subhirtella* 'Autumnalis' and autumn-colouring *P. sargentii* should not be hard pruned, as this spoils the individual line of the spreading branches. If absolutely necessary, take out a whole branch or side branch in late summer.

Laurels: Both Portugal laurel (*Prunus lusitanica*) and cherry laurel (*P. laurocerasus*) are ironclad evergreen survivors of old gardens. They will withstand shade and drought, and rise above it all, frequently making trees 6–8m (20–25ft) tall and seeding themselves around, to the detriment of more delicate competitors. Both species can either be cut back to a framework of stumped branches, or to the ground. In the long run, cutting to the ground is more successful, and there is less likelihood of subsequent die-back. If it is necessary to retain a screen while reducing and rejuvenating the laurels, multi-stemmed plants can be cut down in early spring one side at a time, repeating the operation when growth on the one side has risen sufficiently. (Two years should see 2m (6ft) of growth.) For best results start on the sunniest side. With single-stemmed plants there is no option but to cut the whole thing down in one year.

Pyracantha   Rosaceae
Fire thorn

§ Single- or multi-stemmed shrub
☐ Max. height: 4–5m (12–15ft)
♦ Evergreen
✳ Sun or part shade

An old free-standing pyracantha bent over and laden with berries may be marvellous for a while, but if it is in the way of your gardening, what can you do with it? It is an impossible, spine-riddled tangle, requiring both courage and armour plating to reduce it. Pyracantha is the bougainvillea of the north.

Well, you can chainsaw your way into the trunk, fell it, chop it into blocks of tangle, and try to burn it, close by if possible so that thorns do not get into wheelbarrow tyres. It will almost certainly sprout again, which may suit you. It can then be trained to more modest proportions.

Less massive specimens should have wayward limbs cut out, taking the stumps back within the remaining canopy of the plant. Wall-trained specimens which have rolled over and outwards at the top should have some limbs taken back to the top, and some taken lower down, so that the rush of regrowth is spread over the face of the whole plant, rather than letting it all happen at the top again.

Mixed pyracantha hedge

Pyrus communis in old age

Pyrus   Rosaceae

Pear

§ Single-stemmed tree
▯ Max. height: 8m (25ft)
♦ Deciduous
✽ Sun

Old pears have a lovely weeping, scrolled habit to the branches, and they are worth keeping for their structure and dark bark alone. They are, however, susceptible to gale damage at this stage, and occasional branches may have to be removed in late winter if this occurs. Old pears may also be pollarded in winter, to reduce the height more significantly, but retaining the strength of the trunk.

Old pears required for fruit production are better treated gently, thinning out lightly the density of each branch by perhaps 25–30 percent to let light and air to the fruits, and to reduce the number of fruits and the weight of the branches. Heavy pruning will only promote long watershoots and the need for further pruning.

Quercus   Fagaceae

Oak

§ Single-stemmed tree
▯ Max. height: 30m (100ft)
♦ Deciduous or evergreen
✽ Sun

Oaks are long-lived, light-hungry trees which respond well, if slowly, to heavy pruning. Pruning is best done in winter. On younger trees it is worth trying to prune out one half of double leaders, for the long-term strength of the tree. Fast-growing species like the red oak, *Quercus rubra*, are especially prone to divided leaders.

This and the common oak, *Quercus robur*, are good trees to garden beneath, because they generally have deep roots and minimal surface root, allowing cultivation around them. They make a good high canopy to provide shade for woodland gardening and rhododendrons. They will withstand a great deal of removal of lower branches, gradually, to admit light below.

Evergreen oaks (*Quercus ilex* etc) have a dense, heavy crown and rolling pendulous branches at maturity. It is difficult to grow anything in their shade, and more sensible to give priority to the fine shape of the canopy at the expense of gardening beneath.

The common oak makes an astonishingly rich wildlife habitat, and is therefore especially worth keeping in a garden if possible.

Quercus palustris in autumn

If necessary, old rhododendrons will respond to hard pruning

Rhododendron Ericaceae

Rhododendron and azalea
The genus *Rhododendron* is large and much hybridized. It may be conveniently be divided into three groups.

Species Rhododendrons

Rhododendrons are heavily branched but single-stemmed plants. They can vary in size from alpine species a centimetre or two high, to trees 10–12m (30–40ft) high. They are all plants which – given suitable growing conditions – require nothing more than to be left to get on with it.

The dwarf species in particular need full light to thrive. If they have been overlaid by other plants, the spoiled branches will not regenerate. Cutting back to live wood must suffice, and replacement may be the only aesthetically acceptable option.

The larger shrubby and tree-sized species are most commonly seen in woodland gardens, where the overhead light canopy can give some shelter to early-season flowers. However, too much shade – as found in neglected gardens – will make the plants leggy and bare at the base. Some species such as *Rhododendron arboreum* and the notorious weed *Rhododendron ponticum* will accept hard pruning, sprouting from cut limbs or from a stump. Others, especially the smooth or shiny-barked species, hate pruning into older wood. The way to proceed here is to shorten back wayward limbs in late winter to healthy strong shoots lower down, and wait for them to fill out. It is a slow process.

As a general rule, the rougher the bark of a species, the more likely it is to respond to hard pruning. If in doubt proceed with caution, and never expect a lower, shaded limb to sprout strongly to fill a gap when cut back.

Hybrid Rhododendrons

There are many kinds of rhododendron hybrids. In recent years there has been interest in the compact species like *R. yakushimanum*, and the fine-leaved smooth-barked Thomsonii series. These finer-flowered, more delicate plants are no more responsive to hard pruning than their parent species.

But there are also the common, large-leaved and large-flowered hybrids, sometimes known as the Hardy Hybrids, which are an extremely accommodating race of plants. These can be cut hard back, either to the ground if they are not grafted, or to fat leafless limbs, and they will shoot away hard. Late winter is the time to be making large cuts. Lighter thinning can be carried out in summer, when the plants are in flower. This has the double advantage of letting you spot any sucker growth with the wrong flowers. Today most rhododendrons are not grafted, but in old gardens it pays to assume that they are, and to expect suckers.

Azalea

Azalea is a name used to refer to a number of deciduous and evergreen rhododendrons. The evergreens or Japanese kinds grow to some 60–120cm (2–4ft) and include the Glenn Dale, Kaempferi, Kurume and Vuyk hybrids. The deciduous azaleas are taller,

1–3m (3–10ft) and include the Exbury, Ghent, Knap Hill and Mollis hybrids.

Evergreen species develop a mushroom-shaped crown of small branches spreading from a short single trunk. Cuts into old wood do not usually provoke any response, and old plants are better left to serve their time and then be scrapped, or propagated if they are a favoured or old variety. Evergreen azaleas which have been shaded out until they are almost leafless will not usefully recover and should be scrapped or replaced.

Deciduous azaleas make a multi-stemmed bush. Old but strong-growing plants may have lank stems shortened back in winter by 50 percent, cutting to a live side branch. Some older stems may be taken out altogether. Beware of cutting grafted plants too low, in case the scion dies out in favour of suckers from the rootstock. Check too that the plant is not already a mass of suckers, by inspecting at flowering time. If there is just one lonely branch of the original hybrid left in a bush of suckers, then the battle is as good as lost, and it may be better to settle for the bush of suckers, or to scrap the plant.

In general, deciduous azaleas are happy to get on with life without much pruning so long as they have enough light and moisture. The best approach when dealing with them in neglected gardens is to give them light again by pruning other plants, and to give them a generous organic mulch of old compost or leaf litter. Then allow them time to recover and flower before making life-and-death decisions about them.

Azalea 'Silver Slipper'

Rhus typhina in autumn, showing old trunks and suckers

Rhus   Anacardiaceae
Sumach

§ Single-stemmed shrubs, suckering
☐ Max. height: 6m (20ft)
♦ Deciduous
❋ Sun

The common species, *Rhus glabra* and *R. typhina*, like to make a balanced, well branched dome on a single trunk. In old age they are prone to heave over at the base, or to snap off. Partially disfigured canopies cannot be persuaded to fill out again by pruning, although time and light will help gradually to fill gaps. Heavy pruning is best restricted to the removal in winter of unwanted or misplaced branches back to the trunk. Pruning in expectation of regeneration is successful only in young twigs. Beware of cutting down any large healthy rhus, as suckers will sprout up over a large area and be difficult to kill.

It is sensible to wear gloves when dealing with all species of rhus, since some people show a highly allergic reaction to the sap. (*Rhus toxicodendron* is the American 'poison ivy'.)

Ribes   Grossulariaceae
Flowering Currant

§ Single- or multi-stemmed shrubs
☐ Max. height: 2m (6ft)
♦ Deciduous
❋ Sun or part shade

The common flowering currant, *Ribes sanguineum*, is a tough, easily grown shrub, and like its cousin the gooseberry is a great survivor. It propagates itself by seed and by lay-ering its lowest branches to the ground. Old plants can be pruned down low in winter and for best response should be fed and mulched heavily. They will only miss one season of flower. Very old plants with decay at the root are best discarded and replaced with cuttings, easily rooted as hardwood cuttings in late autumn.

More delicate species like *Ribes odoratum* (perfumed), *R. laurifolium* and *R. speciosum* (which is tender and often grown on walls) should be treated more cautiously, and encouraged into strong health with heavy feeding before cutting.

Ribes speciosum

Robinia   Leguminosae
False Acacia

§ Single-stemmed suckering tree
☐ Max. height: 25m (80ft)
♦ Deciduous
❋ Sun

Robinia pseudoacacia needs full light to ripen its wood, both for flowering and for winter-hardiness. New branches can sprout from surprisingly old wood, and trees damaged by shade or breakage are well worth pruning, in the hope that new branches will arise to fill the space. Old trees have a wonderfully corrugated and stretched bark, which is a virtue in itself. Neglected and smothered trees may also carry a great deal of dead wood, which is better removed to reduce weight. It takes a

Robinia pseudoacacia

very old spreading robinia to cast heavy shade, and it can be a most useful airy screen tree. Root damage from digging, however, can promote suckers.

If a healthy robinia is cut down, fast-growing suckers will arise from the stump and the roots, requiring considerable and often chemical control. On the other hand, if carefully controlled this can result in a fine multi-stemmed tree of straight, vigorous trunks.

The yellow-leaved form 'Frisia' is often grafted, and exceptionally heavy pruning or cutting down low may result in suckers of the ordinary green robinia coming from the base or from the roots further afield. 'Frisia' can happily be pollarded, cutting back the shoots in late winter every two to three years to a framework of branches. This produces especially bright and lush foliage.

Romneya   Papaveraceae
Tree poppy

§   Suckering shrub
☐   Max. height: 2m (6ft)
♦   Deciduous
✱   Sun

Where romneya survives in old gardens, all it requires to be livened up is relieving of overgrowth, cutting down low in early spring, and a hefty feed. Sunshine will do the rest. It will run considerable distances and pass under walls. Do not assume that where you find it is where it was planted.

Rosa   Rosaceae
Rose

§   Multi-stemmed or sucking shrubs
☐   Max. height: 1–10m (3–30ft)
♦   Deciduous
✱   Sun

Roses are not the difficult creatures some would have us believe. They are naturally tough, vigorous plants which will withstand the cruellest pruning, from man or even from a chamois up the mountains.

Weakness in roses comes with old age (20–40 years) and old, constitutionally weak varieties. If a rose is ugly because it is full of dead wood and massive, or ugly because it is just one miserable stick with a single operatic-but-tubercular flower, then heavy winter prun-

Rosa moyesii 'Sealing Wax'

Rubus biflorus

ing (with secateurs or even a bow saw) and heavy feeding are in order. Prune low. If the results are poor over the next season, then the plant should be scrapped and replaced.

If you do take out an old rose, or an old rose bed, remember that because of specific replant disease, or 'rose sickness' as it is commonly known, roses are unlikely to succeed in that soil again. You will need to replace the soil to a depth of 75cm (30in).

Hybrids
A hybrid rose which has a great gnarled rootstock and just a few spindly or ancient stems from it is not worth keeping, except perhaps to try to identify the variety and propagate from it (by cuttings or grafting). Replace it if you like it enough. Cutting down low and heavy feeding frequently has no effect whatsoever on these Sleeping Beauties. A new vigorous specimen will do far more for the garden over the coming years.

Vigorous, strong-growing roses can be fed and pruned hard back and fed again with more success. Watch out to be sure that new growth, as it appears, is not sucker growth from the stock, rather then the desired scion variety.

Species
Species roses can be astonishingly tough and astonishingly large. A rose which has climbed 6m (20ft) up a tree can be cut off low down in winter and expected to survive, although the shock is considerable. The plant often gives a worryingly long pause for thought before taking a deep breath and starting again. The rule with roses should be that if it looks a mess, then it is worth cutting hard to see what happens.

Rosmarinus   Labiatae
Rosemary

§   Multi-stemmed shrubs
☐   Max. height: 1–2m (3–6ft)
♦   Evergreen
✱   Full sun

In free-draining soil, and provided the plant has not been overtaken by shade, rosemary may live for 20 years or more. Unless conditions are going to be sufficiently sunny again there is little point in preserving rosemary. It resents cuts into old wood and does not sprout successfully. It is reluctant to fill holes in the canopy, even when light is readmitted. Nor does it transplant well. But in a sunny place, an old gaunt rosemary can have a great charm, and by the removal of the more wayward outgrowths in late spring, it can be retained as a rather craggy bush by regular seasonal pruning at the edges. Late summer cuttings are easy, and offer the best way of preserving an old plant.

Rubus   Rosaceae
Bramble

§   Suckering shrubs
☐   Max. height: 3m (10ft)
♦   Semi-evergreen
✱   Sun or part shade

All rubus will respond to cutting down low and being given a heavy feeding. Stems are short-lived and the plants are used to shooting again from the base. Some species, like the bramble itself, *Rubus fruticosus*, and pink-flowered *Rubus spectabilis*, can be weeds in large old gardens, and may require chemical control, following initial digging out of the principal roots.

A form of *Salix alba* with good bark, pollarded for winter colour.

Salix   Salicaceae

Willow

§ Large trees to dwarf shrubs
[] Max. height: 10cm–25m (4in–80ft)
♦ Deciduous
✳ Sun

Willows can be a problem and a blessing in old gardens. Frequently you will find self-sown specimens of the goat willow, *Salix caprea*, at 6 and 8m (20–25ft) tall, right in the middle of a border or shrubbery. And while willow is easy and soft to cut down, it also sprouts vigorously from a stump. So any stumps left in must be killed chemically to prevent regrowth.

On the other hand, because willow sprouts so willingly from large wounds, self-sown specimens can be used as a stop-gap in all sorts of ways. Trees of species like *Salix alba*, which may ultimately be far too large for their position, but which come in forms with brightly coloured bark, can be cruelly pollarded and expected quickly to fill out again in an explosion of orange or yellow stems. They can hide a shed, or fill a gap until other things are established. As a quick and temporary screen or shelter belt, willow rods even up to 5cm (2in) across can be cut in winter and simply thrust 60cm (2ft) into the ground to grow. If you have a willow to dispose of, think about whether it has any possible use to you before you burn it.

Sambucus   Caprifoliaceae

Elderberry

§ Single- or multi-stemmed small tree
[] Max. height: 6m (20ft)
♦ Deciduous
✳ Sun or part shade

Sambucus nigra is another weed species of old gardens. If it is in the way, remove it. But do not despise elder because it is common. It has fine flowers and good berries and can fill a gap until other things have been established. Prune elder as hard as you like, to the ground, or to a framework at 2–3m (6–10ft) high if you prefer. You will lose flowers for a couple of years, but so what?

All the fancy forms of elder can be cut just as hard, including the cut-leaved 'Laciniata', the purple-leaved 'Guincho Purple' or the yellow cut-leaved form of the red-berried elder *Sambucus racemosa* 'Plumosa Aurea'. In clearing around elders, remember that the purple form is at its best in full sun, whereas the yellow form may scorch if not given a little shade.

Santolina   Compositae

Cotton lavender

§ Multi-stemmed small shrub
[] Max. height: 1m (3ft)
♦ Evergreen
✳ Full sun

Old specimens of *Santolina chamaecyparissus* and *pinnata* are not common, because they are not long lived, can flower themselves to death and, like most grey-leaved plants, suc-

Sambucus racemosa 'Plumosa Aurea'.

cumb quickly to shade. Ragged young specimens with a 1–2cm ($^{1}/_{2}$–$^{3}/_{4}$ in). trunk may be cut back hard in mid to late spring and expected to shoot out hard. Ragged old specimens with 4–5cm (2in) trunks are hardly worth saving. Replace them with cuttings. The green-leaved *Santolina rosmarinifolia* is less willing to remain compact over four to five years than the greys, even with regular pruning.

Santolina pruned and used as a foliage plant.

Sarcococca   Buxaceae
Sweet box

§ Dense suckering shrubs
⬚ Max. height: 1.5m (5ft)
♦ Evergreen
✱ Sun or part shade

Sarcococca is such a dense-rooting plant that it rarely becomes riddled with weed, even in neglected gardens. It does, however, succumb to too much shade, and frequently all it requires for a new lease of life is clearance around it and a good mulch of old compost. If necessary the colony can be cut down low for the purposes of dealing with an infiltration of herbaceous weed, but this weakens as much as invigorates the plant. Recovery is not quick.

Sequoia   Taxodiaceae
Coast redwood

§ Single-stemmed conifer
⬚ Max. height: 50m (165ft)
♦ Evergreen
✱ Sun

Sequoia sempervirens is one of the world's giant trees. In European gardens it still remains to be seen if the redwood can ever equal the giant stature it has in western America. It seems unlikely. Nevertheless it is a large and fast-growing tree. If the size of its middle age can be accommodated, then all any specimen requires is light. So long as it still has its leader, any youthful specimen may well still make good when

Sequoiadendron giganteum

Skimmia in fruit and flower

freed of smothering competition. In old age its branch structure does not have the graceful sweeping branches of its cousin, *Sequoiadendron*. Tall, exposed specimens may suffer some wind-burn (browning of leaves) from cold winter winds, but it is usually made good the following season. Any dead or largely dead branches may be removed back to the trunk in winter.

Sequoiadendron   (Giant redwood)
Taxodiaceae
Treat as for **Sequoia** (see above)

Skimmia   Rutaceae
Skimmia

§ Dense multi-stemmed shrubs
⬚ Max. height: 2m (6ft)
♦ Evergreen
✱ Sun or shade

When not overlaid by other shrubs, skimmias need no attention at all. However, if they have been disfigured or shaded out by other plants, light and time are the best healers. Very old shrubs can be cut back hard, doing a section at a time over three to four years, to reduce the shock. Older plants may become yellow due to a deficiency in minerals, which can be put right by an application of trace elements.

Sorbaria   Rosaceae
Sorbaria

§ Multi-stemmed or suckering shrubs
⬚ Max. height: 3–4m (10–12ft)
♦ Deciduous
✱ Sun or light shade

Easily grown shrubs which often self-seed on moister soils. Flowering is best in full sun. Very old plants may have the oldest, arched-over stems cut out altogether, to leave the younger ones to develop. Stems of medium age may

be reduced back to a strong shoot, to encourage a more upright habit and more generous flowering. If required all stems may be cut down low in early spring.

Sorbus   Rosaceae
Mountain ash, rowan, whitebeam

§ Trees or shrubs, occasionally suckering
⬚ Max. height: 1– 6m (3–20ft)
♦ Deciduous
✱ Sun

Sorbus are not easy trees to prune. Large wounds commonly lead to die-back, and it is better to remove a branch than to shorten it. Gaps in the canopy do not readily fill out again, but old, gnarled specimens, especially of the common rowan, *Sorbus aucuparia*, have their own appeal. Fireblight (*Erwinia amylovora*) can cause severe die-back, wrecking the statuesque habit of such species as *Sorbus sargentiana*. Sometimes selected clones such as the large-leaved, grey *Sorbus thibetica* 'John Mitchell' may be found to have been grafted on to different stocks which may sucker and suppress the graft itself. Thorn is a common stock for sorbus, and can sucker very badly. All suckers should be removed as soon as possible. Species which themselves sucker (*Sorbus poteriifolia, reducta*, etc) may have the older stems cut out in early spring if required. Heavy feeding is not beneficial.

Sorbus aucuparia thriving in cold upland conditions

Stachyurus praecox

Spartium · Leguminosae

Spanish broom

§ Single-stemmed, twiggy shrubs
☐ Max. height: 3m (10ft)
♦ Semi-evergreen
✳ Full sun

Considering that *Spartium junceum* is in the Legume family, cuts into younger green wood sprout surprisingly well. Old plants become gaunt and leggy, and shade ruins them. Cuts into older, brown-barked wood will not provoke growth and can lead to die-back. Old specimens should either be shortened back in late spring to leave a canopy of what were lower branches, or scrapped and replaced.

Spiraea · Rosaceae

Spiraea

§ Multi-stemmed or suckering shrubs
☐ Max. height: 2–3m (6–10ft)
♦ Deciduous
✳ Sun

Old spiraeas can be cut hard and low with great success. Heavy feeding pays dividends. Colonies of suckering *Spiraea douglasii* may be taken down to a few centimetres in early spring with a chainsaw or brush-cutter, and will flower again the same season. Old plants of many species will be found to be making new roots from the younger, outer stems of the clump. These clumps can be dug up and broken up, using the younger outer parts to make new plants, if required. All the lower, twiggy varieties like 'Anthony Waterer' and 'Goldflame' will benefit from being cut down low in early spring, and well fed and mulched.

Stachyurus · Stachyuraceae

Stachyurus

§ Single-stemmed shrub
☐ Max. height: 3m (10ft)
♦ Deciduous
✳ Sun or dappled shade

Once past its early youth, stachyurus does not like being cut hard or low. Readmit sufficient light, and gently shorten back wayward branches to form an acceptable shape. Then let nature heal. Too much shade will stop it producing its drooping yellow catkins.

Staphylea · Staphyleaceae

Bladder-nut

§ Multi-stemmed shrubs
☐ Max. height: 4–5m (12–15ft)
♦ Deciduous
✳ Sun or part shade

Easily grown shrubs requiring little pruning once established. Readmit enough light to encourage flowering. The habit is frequently congested at the base, and there is no virtue in fighting this. However, a few old stems can be cut right out at the base and their tops careful extricated from the remaining canopy. Take them out one at a time, to be sure that the remaining stems will still be self-supporting without the older trunks to shore them up.

Staphylea pinnata

Stewartia pseudocamellia in old age

Stephanandra · Rosaceae

Stephanandra

§ Suckering shrubs
☐ Max. height: 1–2m (3–6ft)
♦ Deciduous
✳ Sun or part shade

Stephanandra incisa and *S. tanakae* are vigorous, suckering and layering shrubs, but by no means weed-proof. Old colonies may usefully be taken down to 3–5cm (1 ½–2in) in mid-spring with a chainsaw. This will facilitate the chemical treatment of any herbaceous weeds which may have infiltrated the clump. The colony can be dug back to acceptable proportions with a sharp spade, and the root mass removed.

Stewartia · Theaceae

Stewartia

§ Small tree or large shrub
☐ Max. height: 5m (15ft)
♦ Deciduous
✳ Semi-shade

Stewartia pseudocamellia enjoys light shade, especially to its roots, and so is easily overcrowded in neglected gardens. Badly shaped specimens first of all need light to be readmitted, and the removal of any great root competition for moisture. Then a gentle reshaping of the canopy, by taking branches back to a live shoot, should follow. Time will do the rest.

Syringa vulgaris 'Souvenir de Louis Spaeth'

Styrax — Styracaceae
Snowbell, snowdrop tree

§ **Single-stemmed small trees**
▯ **Max. height: 6m (20ft)**
◆ **Deciduous**
✳ **Sun or part shade**

Styrax japonica, the snowdrop tree, makes rather a slender shape, and will lose its lower branches if competition for light and moisture is too great. Once gone, these cannot be replaced by pruning. It is best simply to re-admit sufficient light, prune out any dead or misplaced small branches in late summer, and allow time to fill out the remaining canopy. *Styrax obassia* and *hemsleyana* are rounder-headed trees, and in disfigured specimens it is worth gently shortening back vigorous side branches in late spring to help fill out any holes in the canopy.

Sycopsis — Hamamelidaceae
Treat as for **Hamamelis** (page 114)

Symphoricarpos — Caprifoliaceae
Snowberry

§ **Suckering shrubs**
▯ **Max. height: 2m (6ft)**
◆ **Deciduous**
✳ **Sun or shade**

Symphoricarpos albus, *orbiculatus* and all their hybrids can easily become weed species in neglected gardens, spreading by sucker and layer until they form impenetrable colonies. Removal, if necessary, is by heavy digging and treating the regrowth with chemicals. Old colonies simply requiring rejuvenation can be thinned of old stems, or cut down low in their entirety with a chainsaw in winter or spring. Regrowth is very fast. A spring application of high-nitrogen fertilizer will encourage pruned colonies which grow in particularly dry rooty conditions.

Syringa — Oleaceae
Lilac

§ **Single- or multi-stemmed shrubs**
▯ **Max. height: 5m (15ft)**
◆ **Deciduous**
✳ **Sun or part shade**

Like many another member of the olive family, lilacs will respond well to hard pruning. But hard feeding is just as important, if the regrowth is to be strong.

Old plants of the common lilac, *Syringa vulgaris*, can be singularly dreary and very large. To rejuvenate old plants, cut out all the sucker growth at the base, to force the energy into the desired remaining trunk or trunks. (Occasionally an old lilac may still be found grafted on to privet.) Then in winter reduce the branch structure to a level some 60cm (2ft) below the desired final height. To put a new front on the bush, take a front branch or trunk lower, so that the regrowth will clothe the front of the bush. Strong shoots will appear from buds appearing out of unpromisingly old wood, both close to the cut ends and lower down the plant.

Sucker growth, if present, will almost certainly continue to appear in subsequent years, and it should continue to be removed. However, in cases where the plant is not grafted and the suckers are the same as the main plant, the strongest new stems may be retained to replace older, tired trunks. Flowering will usually recommence in the second year after pruning. If need be, lilacs can be cut right down to regrow, but the problems of suckering are thus aggravated.

The same hard treatment can be given to the other strong-growing species such as *Syringa emodi*, *josikaea*, x *persica*, *reflexa* and the hybrids 'Bellicent', 'Elinor' etc. Once again, beware of encouraging grafted plants to sucker.

The smaller lilacs such as *Syringa meyeri* 'Palibin' and *microphylla* 'Superba' need treating with more caution, but will still respond to heavy pruning.

Tamarix — Tamaricaceae
Tamarisk

§ **Single-stemmed shrubs or small trees**
▯ **Max. height: 5m (15ft)**
◆ **Deciduous**
✳ **Full sun**

Tamarix ramosissima (= *pentandra*) and *tetrandra* are seaside shrubs which revel in sunny, windy conditions. Pamper them with too much food and shelter, and they become uselessly leggy and tall, and often heave themselves over as a result. Sound but rank specimens in sun may be cut hard back in spring to a framework of branches, from which a new branch structure for regular pruning can be developed.

Tamarix ramosissima (syn. *pentandra*)

Taxus baccata at maturity

Taxodium (Swamp cypress)

Taxodiaceae
Treat as for **Picea** (page 125)

Taxus Taxaceae

Yew

§ Single-stemmed tree
☐ Max. height: 13m (45ft)
♦ Evergreen
✳ Sun or shade

Taxus baccata can be an exceptionally long-lived tree which, during its lifetime, may have had two or three branch structures regrown from the trunk. Hard pruning of the entire tree back to the trunk is possible in winter with good results.

In the heavy shade of deciduous trees, yew will often seed itself, coming into its own when the deciduous trees die. However, yews which were once woodland understorey and have suddenly, through the clearance of other trees, become the woodland canopy itself, can be prone to wind-throw. It may be beneficial on trees 5–10m (15–30ft) tall to shorten back the canopy by a third or more in late winter, to ensure they remain stable while further supporting roots are established.

A mature yew which overhangs and smothers a garden or building can, if required, have the offending face of the tree cut back in winter to the trunk or vertical branches. The entire side of the tree can be regrown, as you might for hedging yews. In exposed positions, care should be taken when doing this not to destabilize the tree.

Yew has greedy shallow roots, making it difficult to garden beneath one. Think carefully before removing the lowest branches of a yew and exposing the ground below.
See also **Hedges** (pages 140–143)

Thuja (Western red cedar)

Cupressaceae
Treat as for **Chamaecyparis** (page 104)

Tilia Tiliaceae

Lime, linden

§ Single-stemmed tree
☐ Max. height: 30m (100ft)
♦ Deciduous
✳ Sun

Limes can be exceptionally long-lived trees, due in part to their ability to regrow from the ground. 1200–1400 year-old specimens of *Tilia cordata,* the small-leaved lime, exist in northern England, having regrown from the base several times. Limes will also withstand heavy pruning of their branches in winter, making them especially successful as pollard trees.

In some species the great attraction is in the tall-domed habit, and it would be a shame to cut back a fine specimen of weeping silver lime, *Tilia petiolaris,* which has such good pendulous clouds of foliage.

On the other hand, the common lime, *Tilia x europaea,* is a frequent tree in old gardens, fast-growing, shallow-rooting, happy in industrial pollution, and casting dense shade. Even heavy-limbed specimens can be cut hard back in winter, to a structure of open branches, and allowed to regrow either as a long-term tree, or as a pollard for regular re-cutting. By this means it is possible to admit light below, and to reduce the moisture requirements of the tree. *Tilia platyphyllos* 'Rubra' has red winter twigs which are seen to best effect in a regime of regular cutting.

Old limes are frequently found with a mass of epicormic shoots clustered like a crow's nest around the trunk. These can all be cut away in early spring. They will always regrow, but cutting late (just before leaf-break) and cutting close to the trunk will reduce the opportunity for regrowth in any season.

Ulex Leguminosae

Gorse

§ Single-stemmed twiggy shrubs
☐ Max. height: 3m (10ft)
♦ Deciduous
✳ Full sun

Shade and shelter ruin gorse bushes. They are happiest in full exposure to sun and wind, often beside the sea, and grazed by passing animals to keep them dense. Old gorse plants which have become bare at the base will not respond to hard pruning. They are better discarded and replaced either with new plants, or with something more comely. Occasionally the double form *Ulex europaeus* 'Flore Pleno' is found in gardens. It is more garden-worthy, but just as hard to manage. Old gorse bushes which are retained should be well clipped into the soft wood only after flowering – grazed – to keep them dense.

Ulmus Ulmaceae

Elm

§ Single-stemmed tree
☐ Max. height: 30m (100ft)
♦ Deciduous
✳ Sun

Despite the ravages of Dutch elm disease in western Europe, elms can still be found in gardens, as suckers arising from old root systems. Commonly these suckers survive until they are 4–6m (12–20ft) tall, when the trunks are reinfected with the fungus by beetles burrowing beneath the bark. They may seem perfectly healthy, and it is tempting to consider theses trees as a long-term part of the garden. Then suddenly one year, they lose leaf and die. It is a mistake to make any plans around elms at present. Fell and burn diseased trunks.

Viburnum Caprifoliaceae

Viburnum

§ Single- or multi-stemmed shrubs
☐ Max. height: 1–4m (3–12ft)
♦ Deciduous or evergreen
✳ Sun or part shade

Deciduous species like *Viburnum opulus, plicatum, farreri* and x *bodnantense* can all be cut down low in early spring if really necessary,

Viburnum x bodnantense

and they will regrow quickly. Huge specimens of the finer-twigged ones like *farreri* and x *bodnantense* are better cut back and thinned, because cutting right down often produces a forest of thin, whippy stems which need careful thinning and selection to make a strong new shrub. *Viburnum plicatum* is known for the poise of its branches, which are held almost horizontal in some forms. These forms make ugly, angular growth when heavily pruned back, and the winter silhouette is best served by cutting the whole plant low and regrowing it, rather than nibbling at the branches.

The evergreen species, including *Viburnum carlesii*, *rhytidophyllum* and *tinus*, will sprout surprisingly well from cuts made into branches 2–3cm (1in) across in spring. Heavier pruning brings an increasingly smaller response. Shortening back over a few years is always better then pruning right down.

Look out for suckers on old grafted plants and remove them at the base. *Viburnum lantana* is often used for a stock under *Viburnum* x *burkwoodii*, x *carlcephalum* and x *juddii*.

Vitis   Vitaceae
Vine

§ **Single-stemmed climbers**
☐ **Max. height: 10m (30ft)**
♦ **Deciduous**
✳ **Sun**

As well as the grapevine, *Vitis vinifera,* and its fancy forms such as the purple-leaved 'Purpurea' and dusky 'Incana', there are also rampant ornamental vines such as *Vitis amurensis* and *coignetiae*. All will survive and even thrive in the chaos of a neglected gar-

Vitis coignetiae

Wisteria

den. They can all be pruned hard back in early winter (later cutting makes the wounds bleed) and will regrow quickly. Feeding and mulching is beneficial.

Weigela   Caprifoliaceae
Weigela

§ **Multi-stemmed shrub**
☐ **Max. height: 2–3m (6–10ft)**
♦ **Deciduous**
✳ **Sun or part shade**

Weigelas will withstand a great deal of drought and shade, and are great survivors in old gardens. However, given better conditions, they offer much better results. They will produce a whole new branch structure in a couple of years if they are cut down low in early spring, well fed and mulched, and given enough light. Or they can be thinned out in winter, removing dead wood and crossing branches, and letting in the light and air to encourage new wood. Again, feed well and mulch.

Wisteria   Leguminosae
Wisteria

§ **Single-stemmed climber**
☐ **Max. height: 25m (80ft)**
♦ **Deciduous**
✳ **Full sun**

Old wisterias which have grown into deciduous trees can usually be allowed to remain. Cutting them back below the tree's canopy will reduce flowering.

Old wisterias on walls can have some of the heavier wood thinned away in winter if it is felt necessary, and younger stems trained into their place. The aim should be to get a

structure close to the wall once more, from which annual pruning can take place.

Occasionally it is the stem itself, close to the ground, which is the problem. It may have swung out in a loop from the wall and gradually developed into a heavy trunk, blocking the path. Even these main stems can be cut through in winter with some success. More often than not a bud will break at or below ground level. Try to cut no closer than 30cm (12in) from the ground, so there are more dormant buds left to show willing. Heavy watering through the first summer ensures good growth.

Yucca   Agavaceae
Adam's needle

§ **Multi-stemmed shrub**
☐ **Max. height: 3m (10ft)**
♦ **Evergreen**
✳ **Full sun**

Not all *yuccas* make a stem. Of those that do, *Yucca gloriosa* is the best known. Once a rosette has flowered it begins to produce a circle of smaller rosettes around its base. These grow on and flower, until gradually a massive, interlocking clump is formed. Where such a clump needs a little restructuring, cut out the oldest, flowered stems in late spring, giving space and air to the remainder, so they can show off their form and receive sufficient sun to ripen and flower. Stems shortened to a branch produce a much less attractive outline than cutting to the base.

Yucca

Heaths and Heathers

The dwarf, shrubby members of the Ericaceae collectively known as heathers include species of *Calluna* and *Daboecia* as well as *Erica*.

Most neglected heather gardens succumb quickly to weeds and grass. It is usually best to start again or do something different. In any case most heathers are not long lived in a garden situation. Rich garden soils and shelter produce a luxurious but brief lifespan. Shade is their coup de grace. Many heathers have outlived their tidiness in 10 years. Some will last 30 with regular clipping and a suitably mean soil. But with neglect, heathers quickly pass beyond being saveable. The tree heath, *Erica arborea* is the exception to the rule, and sprouts well from large cuts or from ground level.

Acid-loving *Calluna vulgaris* (ling, Scotch heather), the common late summer heather of the British moorlands, is much used in its cultivated forms in heather gardens. Cuts into one- and sometimes two-year-old wood will produce new shoots, but cuts into older wood produce nothing. Once a *calluna* has become bald at the centre and leggy – 30–60cm (1–2ft) depending on the variety – there is no recovering it. Scrap it and replace it.

Heather and conifer gardens – the whole point is their freshness. Bald, leggy plants are better scrapped.

Like *callunas* and *daboecias*, all *ericas* (*Erica arborea* excepted) quickly become shabby without annual pruning. If they are infested with weeds, or leggy and bare at the centre, they are better replaced. Frequently there will be layers which have rooted themselves, and these can be detached in early spring or autumn to make new plants. *E. carnea*, *E. x darleyensis*, and *E. vagans* are all lime-tolerant.

Erica arborea becomes sprawling and misshapen in old age, and is often broken or sprained by snow. It can be cut off at ground level and will regrow with great success. Expect 1.5–2m (5–6ft) of new growth in two years.

Erica arborea 'Alpina' – mature plants up to 4m (12ft) tall can be cut right down with good results.

Erica vagans begins to climb into a blue spruce. Let them blend but not disfigure each other.

The life of *calluna* is usefully prolonged by regular clipping (done by sheep and deer on the moors) to make it bushy. Clip off the very tips of the shoots (it will break your heart) just as they show colour and shoot in spring. If you can spare the time, clip them over again lightly after flowering. Miss this clipping in the first couple of years, and you establish the road to a bald centre far sooner. Golden forms demand even more light than the greens to stay densely leafy. The grey forms are yet more demanding.

Acid-loving *Daboecia cantabrica*, St. Dabeoc's heath, is the largest flowered of the low heathers at 30–50cm (12–20in), and the most lax in growth. Without annual pruning back of the long flower stems, plants quickly become swirling pools of slumped, dead and live foliage.

Included in the genus *Erica* are the low winter-flowering *Erica carnea* (alpine heath or winter heath) and *E. cinerea* (bell heather), knee-high *E. vagans* (Cornish heath) and *E. x darleyensis*, and the hardy tree heather *Erica arborea* 'Alpina'.

Hedges

Old Hedges

There are several reasons for needing to cut back an old hedge. It may be balding and patchy, and so fat at the top that the lower half receives no light and has died out. It may have become riddled with ivy or brambles.

The good thing about hedges, however, is that they are used to being cut, and most will respond well to hard pruning. In a smart, precise garden it may be necessary to get back to crisp clean lines and right angles. In a cottage garden it may only be necessary to restore an even profile and consistent screen.

Even well-tended hedges frequently become too tall or fat over the years, and therefore difficult to clip. But think hard about cutting back a hedge simply because it is large. If it is taking up three quarters of an adjoining path, then you have good reason to cut. But if it is attractively or usefully big – if it is one of those wonderful, fat, rolling cloud-formations of yew or holly – then spare it if you can. Make use of its size. It will lend untold dignity to your garden. It may be difficult and slow to clip, but it is not necessarily coming to any harm in itself. It may even be worth moving a path to accommodate it.

Pruning Hedges

A fuller explanation of the rejuvenation of the main types of hedge follows below, but it is useful to look first at the principles of rejuvenating any hedge.

1 To get a dense and closely textured hedge, full light will be necessary. Other trees and shrubs may need pruning first to allow the hedge to flourish. Hedges running under the canopy of trees will always struggle and require extra feeding and watering to get them back into shape.

2 Starved hedges never respond to cutting as well as well-fed ones. Life is tough enough in a hedge as it is, and suddenly to make large amounts of new growth requires plentiful energy and food. Help it along. Feed it generously.

3 You must think about the future profile of the hedge before you cut. Ideally a hedge will have sides which slope together slightly at the top, to receive maximum light, but this is not absolutely vital. One thing is certain, however: bald patches low down will never refill without letting in good light from above. It is usually more satisfactory to cut back the whole hedge than to start cutting back patches.

When you lower the height of a hedge you need to make your cuts at least 30cm (12in) below the future top profile, to ensure that there is space to develop a new twiggy canopy above.

4 Some hedges can be rejuvenated a side at a time, so that the screening value is never lost. Others are better cut down to the ground. Whichever method you choose, you want the maximum growing season available to those new shoots, to race away in spring like greyhounds from a trap, and also to slow down and ripen again in late summer, so the frost does not spoil sappy growth in autumn. Fast-sprouting hedges like privet and hawthorn can be cut in late winter, so that new buds have formed ready for the growing season in spring. Yew and box are better cut in spring, just before growth is about to start, and after the worst frosts are over.

5 The heavy pruning of old hedges is not without risk. Sometimes one or a few of the plants within the hedge never recover and will need replacing with new ones. It is a risk worth taking. The chances are that the plants that died were failing anyway, from the trials of hedge life, and that they would have died soon anyway. Often when you cut back an old hedge you find several plants which have been dead for years, slowly and invisibly smothered by more competitive neighbours.

6 It is possible to insert new plants into gaps in old hedges. A generously prepared hole is essential to give the young plant a chance amongst established plants which have already been fighting each other for any scrap of nutrition. It may be necessary to cut through roots of neighbouring hedging plants to get the hole out but it is a price worth paying to get the new additions off to a good start. The most succfessful new plants are those which are added to hedges which have also been cut back. The extra light gives them much more of a fighting chance. Additions of holly, yew and thorn are more successful than beech, cypress or privet.

Dig out any dead plants in the hedge.

Don't leave stumps – cut back to the trunk.

An old trunk 12 months after cutting back.

Yew Hedges

The yew (*Taxus baccata*) is an astonishingly tough tree. It is resistant to honey fungus. It can survive for thousands of years. It can live in full sun and in almost complete shade. And in sun it makes the tightest of ever-green hedges.

Best of all, it withstands heavy pruning. Remove half a yew's canopy, – reduce a mature tree to a totem pole – and it says, 'Ah well – a bit short of leaf today. But tomorrow and in another 100 years...oh, no!' Which is most convenient for gardeners with old yew hedges in need of serious attention. The yew's powers of regeneration are miraculous.

It is sometimes said that it benefits a yew hedge to be cut hard back every 70 years, to guarantee a completely tight canopy about its trunks. If you do decide that a 70-year period is now up, look first at its general health. Is it on its last legs, and dying out in patches? Is it growing hard but just too big? Is it just a bit bald at the bottom?

If you feel it's weak, then before you start cutting – preferably a whole year before you start cutting – feed the hedge with a general fertilizer, and a mulch of compost. If it's a dry year, soak it occasionally too. Get it in good heart before you start giving it a hard time.

Begin for preference on the side which gets most light and sun. In spring, when the heavy frosts are past and growth is just about to start, saw off all the growth on one side of the hedge, taking it right back to the trunks. Do not be tempted to leave horizontal twiggy bits sticking out; cut back to the verticals. It should feel rather like filleting a fish, except that you keep the bones – the upright trunks and branches – and throw the flesh away. It's a filthy job, and there will be mountains of old twiggy branches to dispose of (they burn marvellously easily if dry). While you are about it, clear out all the water-repelling piles of old dead needles in the bottom of the hedge, until you can see soil again. Once again, feed it (a high-nitrogen fertilizer this time) and mulch it and soak it. Then just wait. Within 12 months the trunks should have clothed themselves from top to bottom in new green shoots.

You are now ready to tackle the top. I like to wait two years before doing this, although if the response to the first cutting has been gener-ous you can proceed the very next year. In spring again, cut off the whole of the top of the hedge. You must take it down to 30cm (12in) below the future level of the hedge, to allow it to make a new twiggy

top within the desired profile. You will find that you may be cutting through trunks the thickness of your wrist in a hedge which has never before been stopped at a lower level, but don't worry about it. All will be well. Feed it, mulch it, water it, and wait again.

Cutting the leading shoots out of any plant always induces vigorous growth at the top and in the side-shoots, and you will find the response to this satisfactorily fast. In another 12 months you will be able to cut back the last side, again taking it right back to the trunks. Over a period of five or six years you can have a completely rejuve-nated hedge tight, healthy and manageable once again

Sometimes, when you begin to cut the first side, you may find that there is no strong central trunk to each hedging plant, but only a bun-dle of thinner ones. If the stems are weak, I prefer to cut the lot down to 20cm (8in) from the ground and regrow it completely, selecting one strong shoot to be the new trunk. Over five to six years you will still get back your tight, full-grown hedge, but in the interim you will lose the screening and shelter value of the hedge.

The lesson here is that, when growing a new yew hedge from scratch, it is valuable to keep the individual plants to single leaders until they make full height, for the sake of future maintenance.

The first side of the hedge is cut away.
Note the old clipping level inside the hedge.

Box Hedges

Unlike yew, box (*Buxus sempervirens*) has a marked ability to put out new shoots around the ends of the bald stumps of side branches, and of considerable diameter. Hedges and topiary can be reduced to an ugly assemblage of chopped limbs and they will still reclothe themselves, poodle-like at first, gradually conjoining to make a whole canopy. However this drastic way of cutting is most successful when the whole plant is cut at the same time. Taking one half severely back first often simply forces the energy of the plant into the remaining green limbs, while the cut half remains leafless.

Box hedges large and small can be cut right down also, if necessary. But beware of doing this to the dwarf box, *Buxus sempervirens* 'Suffruticosa'. It is very slow to grow, and will take many years, even for an established hedge, to get back to 30–40cm (12–16in). It may be better in this case to cut it a side at a time, as for yew hedges. This also lets you deal with weed infestations satisfactorily.

Box cut down to a few centimetres quickly regrows. This is easily enhanced by a good feed and regular mulching.

Box hedging which is generally tired can be given a new sparkle by feeding well, and by working through the outer 10cm (4in) of canopy with finger and thumb in spring, breaking out evenly perhaps 25–30 percent of the canopy, to thin it out and let light and air inside.

Why do anything to a lovely old box hedge like this? Is it coming to any harm?

Beech and Hornbeam Hedges

Beech (*Fagus sylvatica*) and hornbeam (*Carpinus betulus*) both make strong hedges and are inclined to become far too wide for easy clipping. They can be cut like yew, over a period of years in late winter, tackling first one side, then the top, then the other side. But it is better not to cut the branches right back to the trunk. Instead take them back as far as you can to the last little inside bit of leafy twig. Beech and (less so) hornbeam are less willing than yew to produce new buds out of old wood and a remaining live twig can work wonders. Sometimes you may find that a good deal of the new growth comes backwards through the trunks, from branches on the opposite side of the hedge. This is not ideal, but it is better than having no response at all.

Privet Hedges

Most privet hedges (*Ligustrum ovalifolium*) consist of multi-stemmed plants. It is possible to cut down one side at a time in early spring. The aim is not to keep the old trunks at all, but to cut down low the stems which form one side of the hedge. They will quickly sprout away, sometimes making full size again in the first year on smaller hedges. When the first side has regenerated, the other side can be taken down the following spring. Heavy feeding makes a worthwhile difference.

Alternatively, if the screening value can be spared for a year or two, privet responds very well to being wholly cut down low. (Evergreen *Lonicera nitida* can be treated in the same way.) Hard-pruned privet will grow back to waist height in one season, and to achieve better density in the new hedge, it is good idea to stop out the new stems a few times on their way back up to full height.

Conifer Hedges

Conifers make fast and easy hedges. The species most commonly used are the Leyland cypress (x *Cupressocyparis leylandii*) and its golden forms, Lawson's cypress (*Chamaecyparis lawsoniana*), and western cedar (*Thuja plicata*).

The commonest problem of conifer hedges is that they have been allowed to develop into tall, unstoppable screens instead of manageable hedges. The Leyland cypress is notorious for its speed of growth, which may be convenient in the very early years, but is embarrassing soon afterwards. It requires regular clipping at least once a year, right from the outset, to keep a tight hedge of it.

It is possible to take the top out of a cypress hedge, by sawing through the leaders when as much as 10–15cm (4–6in) across. But the hedge almost never looks sleek again. The top (messy if you have to look down on to it) sometimes throws a new leader, but more often it forces up one of its upper side-branches, making a new off-centre leader. Soon this can be growing as fast as the first leader, although dieback from the cut to the main stem often weakens it.

Bald and brown patches low down on a cypress hedge, which have been shaded out by bulging upper branches, cannot be cut back for regeneration. Nor can the sides of the trees be taken back to the trunk to regrow, as you can with yew. The best hope is to thin and shorten back the bulging midriff, *cutting into young wood only*, and then to allow time and light to make what improvements they can.

In a word, a moth-eaten or distended old cypress hedge is bad news. Live with it for as long as you feel you can, then replace it. It is a big, messy job, better done early on while you are making plenty of mess. The soil below will be most impoverished, and in need of plenty of compost or manure before any useful replanting can take place.

Before you remove a poor or overgrown coniferous hedge altogether, consider whether it might have value simply as a loose windbreak. You might informally chop and prune the top to stop it getting unmanageably taller, but let the sides thicken to produce an informal roly-poly screen. Even needle-bearing conifers such as hemlock (*Tsuga heterophylla*) can be used this way to good effect, shearing them roughly every couple of years. (An old beech or holly hedge could be treated the same way.) There may be a good deal of ladder work to keep such a screen in hand, but at least it is quick, rough work, and using secateurs it can be left for a couple of years without attention.

Holly Hedges

Holly (*Ilex aquifolium*) is one of the best plants for a shade-tolerant hedge. Holly hedges which have gaps at the base can have new, very young hollies interplanted to fill the gaps. (Older plants are more expensive and less successful.) They will take a year or two to settle down in such difficult conditions, but they will nevertheless thrive and do their job.

Leyland cypresses, in green or gold can make good fast hedges.

Beech and hemlock, roughly clipped into baffles, keep low-level winds out of this Scottish garden.

Holly hedges showing signs of die-back and thin, poor growth are better cut to the ground than shortened back. This applies even to mature free-standing holly trees with trunks as much as 30–60cm (12–24in) across at the base. Regrowth from ground level is rapid, even in shade. But cutting back large heavy limbs often leads to die-back, and the response is always slower than from ground level.

Mixed Hedges

Mixed beech and hornbeam hedges can be treated as for beech hedges.

There are also more seriously mixed hedges such as you might find in rural areas as a stock-proof boundary hedge. Typically, such a hedge might contain hawthorn, sloe, ash, holly, guelder rose and wild roses. If such a hedge needs to be cut back or cut down, or even to have a significant number of gaps planted up, it is sensible to keep stock away from the hedge for a few years with a wire fence. It needs to be far enough away to prevent stock reaching over to take the new shoots and, whatever the animal, they always seem to have a longer reach than you think.

Alternatively, the traditional method of rejuvenating such hedges is to 'lay' them, by cutting most of the branchwork away, and slashing almost right through the vertical trunks. They can them be bent down low into the line of the hedge. These horizontals are fixed on position with a 'fence' of staked and twisted stems, and then new vertical stems arise from the horizontal trunks into the framework of the fence. It is a considerable skill, and when the job is well done it is delightful to see. But for most of us it is easier an not unaffordable to erect a wire fence for a few years. Indeed, where farm animals and gardens meet, stock-proofing should always use belt and braces. A hedge alone without wire is rarely to be trusted.

Herbaceous Plants

Herbaceous plants form the decoration and 'soft furnishings' of a garden and are therefore not directly in the scope of this book. However it is worth mentioning their place in neglected gardens.

In a benignly neglected garden, just muddling along, all but the feeblest herbaceous plants can be revived by division in spring and replanting in well-dug, generously enriched soil. If you put them back in the same tired but un-enriched soil they will improve, but far more slowly. Be prepared to throw away or give away volumes of the more dominant herbaceous plants. Keep only the strongest off-sets for replanting.

Resist the temptation to wallpaper all parts the garden with a recurring pattern of the same few much-divided herbaceous plants. Equally, do not be afraid to use them boldly, perhaps filling a border or making a long edging with just one plant, until you have time and funds to do something more varied.

Above all, do not be afraid to get on and move, and to really *use* herbaceous plants. They are surprisingly obliging.

When herbaceous plants have become infested with perennial weeds such as ground elder, they become a kind of sanctuary for the weed, a place where you may not safely use weedkiller.

There are two possible solutions to this problem. You can lift the plant in spring and divide it into pieces so small that you can confidently say there is no weed root left in there. Washing the roots clean with a hose is sometimes helpful. Plant these off-sets elsewhere, in clean soil, where they can build up again into good clumps, while you deal ruthlessly and efficiently with the weeds in their old home.

Or you can try to treat the weeds *in situ* with a weedkiller applied directly to their leaves only. With care it can be done, and with something like bindweed which lingers so, it is often inevitably the only way to achieve the final clean-up, even after clearance and replanting. Remember however, that an old weak clump of anything, be it ever so weed-free, is no use in a garden. Division and feeding is just as important as cleanliness.

In gardens which have progressed much further down the primrose path to dusky neglect, most of the herbaceous plants will have succumbed long since to shade, drought and root competition. Grass and trees eat them for breakfast.

But there are always a few survivors. Those bulbs which are natural woodlanders survive well enough. And there are plants such as peonies and Solomon's seal (*Polygonatum* x *hybridum*) which will survive for years in rank grass or heavy shade.

Paeonia officinalis 'Rubra Plena'

Even peonies, although they are well known for their dislike of disturbance, will benefit from spring division (still into sizeable clumps) and replanting in a rich new hole after standing in the same soil for 30 or 40 years. Think of some dry old Anita Brookner heroine going on a second honeymoon: surviving is fine, but there are better things in life.

The prize for tenacity must surely go to the lily family Liliaceae. Looking at this family as a whole, without the hindsight of recent botanical splittings, it includes almost all the great survivors of abandoned gardens, – daffodils, hostas, certain species of lily, day lilies, lily of the valley, veratrums, butcher's broom, bluebells, dog's-tooth violets and snowdrops. Was there ever a greater catalogue of herbaceous old stagers? Well, okay, add in golden rod, oriental poppies and a few more bulbs and there you have it.

The presence of these plants in old gardens is a great help in the detective work leading to an understanding of what was where in the past. Peonies usually mark the presence of old flower beds (the hybrids do not normally self-seed), where presumably the soil was once good. Solomon's seal, lily of the valley and fancy ferns will indicate that there has been a shady woodland garden here.

The fact that these plants have survived for so long untended means they are naturally tough. Sometimes they may be dwindling, and on their last legs. More often they are the tip of an iceberg of promise. Three or four stems of martagon lilies will, on inspection, be the miserable superstructure of a bucketful of starved bulbs, just waiting to be lifted in early spring, divided and put into some decent soil. In thrree or four years you could have a thriving colony again. Veratrums do the same, lurking in great starved clumps under the soil, ripe for splitting.

Lily of the valley tends to run into corners and hide when it is hungry, making dense plates of root with few enough leaves or flowers above. Slap on a heavy layer of manure or compost, and see them come running. In a couple of years you will be able to see just how much clump there is to divide.

Polygonatum biflorum

Solomon's seal also makes great plates of fat rhizomes underground, crossing backwards and forwards over itself (like a hosta) until if suffers from drought almost more than starvation. If you lift an old clump, it can be broken into scores of individual pieces, every one of which will grow away fast in some fresh soil. The outer, fatter-budded rhizomes will of course establish faster, but even the old inner parts of the clump will make good in a couple of years.

Ruscus aculeatus

Semi-shrubby members of the lily famil, include the *Ruscus* species or butcher's brooms. They are shade-loving plants. In old gardens *Ruscus hypoglossum* can be found as broad evergreen clumps a yard across even in the dry shade of yews or beeches. These can, if you wish, be divided in spring into a dozen still sizeable clumps, for planting elsewhere. Neither this plant nor its more common brother *Ruscus aculeatus* enjoys being divided into very small pieces. Be generous with them if you can.

In cooler and sometimes moister gardens, where ferns are happy, they will survive to a great age. The royal fern, *Osmunda regalis*, will happily live for 100 years or more. But ferns also self-sow prolifically. The presence of common species of fern such as the male fern, lady fern, or broad buckler fern does not mean that they were deliberately planted there. Fancy ferns on the other hand – those with fantastically crimped and tasselled fronds – are a good indicator of previous gardening on that spot. A large crown of an old fern will produce some majestic fronds, given a good scattering of slow-release fertilizer such as bonemeal and a generous mulch of old compost.

Small ferns move easily enough. Often, to show off their form to best advantage, ferns need spacing out by the removal of younger self-sown plants. Even old plants can be moved, taking up an enormous pancake of fibrous root in spring, just as the new fronds are showing signs of beginning to expand.

Topiary

The principal subjects chosen for topiary are box (*Buxus*) and yew (*Taxus*), because they are dense, relatively slow-growing and evergreen. Other plants occasionally encountered include privet (*Ligustrum*), hollies (and especially the small-leaved species like *Ilex crenata*), osmanthus and even *Muehlenbeckia complexa*, a small-leaved scrambling shrub with stems like tangles of black wire. In fact, any evergreen that is densely twiggy and will withstand heavy clipping can be used for topiary.

Cutting of these various species can be found under their separate alphabetical entries. See also **Hedges** (pages 140–143). But it is useful here to look at the general principles of rejuvenating topiary.

It is a generally accepted principle that hedges stay denser low down if the sides slope outwards to catch the light. How then must topiary fare, with many three-dimensional shapes having a dark underside as well as a top and sides? The answer is that some species (box and yew are best) will manage to produce a dense face from clipping

Topiary is about line, light, shade and the irony of plants pretending to geometry. If its imperfections offend you, erect some sculpture instead.

Character or chaos? Topiary with middle-aged spread is surely still acceptable?

even in shade. But the less shade the better. These shapes have been hard-won, and their future needs careful consideration.

So in looking at an old topiary piece, ask yourself these questions. Is the shape a problem? If it is clipped but fat and sagged, does that matter visually, or is that part of its charm and its history? Does it speak to you, for better or worse, of a century of loving gardening? If so you may not need to cut it. Or is it so sagged that it is about to break up and in need of emergency pruning?

Is its shape delightfully sagged, but simply not what you require in your Italianate 'designer' reworking of the garden? In this case also you will need to cut.

The easiest topiary to rejuvenate is that which has been grown on a strong trunk and set of main branches. Box and yew topiary can, if really in a mess, be cut back to these, and the shapes reformed either by eye or inside a metal framework. Or you can simply adjust the shapes to accommodate the problem, increasing the profile on one side to match an accidental increase on the opposite side. It is always easier to increase the shape of a topiary piece than shorten it back a little.

There may be a problem at ground level, where grass has spoiled the canopy, or where ivy has wormed its way in to the tree. Always remember that if you lift the skirts of a topiary piece by cutting, it will

be a long slow business getting them to grow down to ground level again. And if you cut back the underneath surface of a three-dimensional shape, it will be even more difficult to produce a new tight surface. Take it all very slowly. It is worth spending an hour to get out the ivy, when the alternative is years of waiting to regrow a tight shape.

Topiary which has not been cut for years, and has become an assemblage of unrecognizable shapes, offers a simpler choice of action. It can either be clipped in its new amorphous shape or allowed to grow out altogether. Or it can be cut hard and reformed into such new topiary shapes as you may now choose. (If you are anxious to discover the old profile, it is always still there inside the plant, and pruning back one side of the plant will expose the old lines, like a section of a boiled egg.)

Whichever way you choose to proceed, old topiary pieces will benefit enormously from being given adequate light and generous feeding and mulch. In late spring a dressing of high-nitrogen fertilizer such as sulphate of ammonia will spur on hard-pruned specimens.

Almost any evergreen can be topiarised – even the blue Atlas cedar – here turned into a mock espalier.

Useful Names and Addresses

Organizations and Societies

The Garden History Society
77 Cowcross Street
London EC1 6BP
0171 608 2409

The GHS is a learned society which, along with English Heritage, advises local government on planning issues affecting historic parks and gardens. It also has 2000 members, and organizes tours within Britain and abroad, lectures and conferences. A good source of help and advice for those with a more major garden, or those looking for period authenticity.

Association of Garden Trusts
8 Glasshouse Lane
Kenilworth
Warwickshire CV8 2AJ
01926 852976

The best place to find out if there is a County Garden Trust in your area. These lively, regional membership organizations are keen to promote and conserve good gardens and especially historic gardens locally. A useful place to meet people who can 'read' an old garden from its remains.

Royal Horticultural Society
80 Vincent Square
London SW10 2PE
0171 834 4333

Britain's gardening charity now has 250,000 members, for whom technical help and advice is available via post or telephone, or in person at the Society's regional gardens and at many of the shows it runs up and down Britain. Members may borrow books from its London-based Lindley Library through the post. The Society's excellent journal *The Garden* is produced monthly. The subscription is well worthwhile.

NCCPG (National Council for the Conservation of Plants and Gardens)
The Pines
RHS Garden
Wisley
Woking
Surrey GU23 6QP
01483 211465

Despite its title, NCCPG's prime interest is in plants. It is the body which designates the National Collections of individual genera or varieties. Regional Groups are a good place to find interesting plants and knowledgeable gardeners.

Irish Garden Plant Society
c/o National Botanic Gardens
Glasnevin
Dublin 9
Eire

Ireland's equivalent of the NCCPG, taking an especial interest in Irish plants.

Henry Doubleday Research Association (HDRA)
Ryton Organic Gardens
Ryton on Dunsmore
Coventry
West Midlands CV8 3LG
01203 303517

HRDA is the focus for all matters to do with organic gardening. It has a great deal of useful advice to offer, even to those who do not garden entirely on organic principles.

The Wildlife Trusts
The Green
Witham Park
Waterside South
Lincolnm LN5 7JR
01522 544400

The place to find out where your local Wildlife Trust is. These regional trusts bring together all kinds of local experts, whose company may prove helpful. They also offer professional advice and wildlife survey services.

Society of Garden Designers
6 Borough Road
Kingston upon Thames
Surrey KT26BD
0181 974 9483

SGD has many of the major garden designers amongst its membership. Along with local word of mouth, it is a good place to start looking if you need the sevices of a professional designer.

British Association of Landscape Industries
Lanscape House
Henry Street
Keighley
West Yorkshire BD21 3DR
01535 606139

BALI sets the standards for industry-approved contractors. For larger garden construction operations you may wish to choose a contractor from a recommended list.

Association of Professional Landscapers
Creighton Lodge
Hollington Lane
Stramshall
Uttoxeter
Staffordshire ST14 5ES
01889 507256

Tree Helpline 0897 161147 £1.50 per minute
c/o/ Forestry Authority
Alice Holt Lodge
Wrecclesham
Farnham
Surrey GU10 4LF
01420 23337

Thie premium-rate (£1.50 a minute) Helpline offers top-quality professional advice on arboricultural matters. There are also useful Arboricultural Practice Notes available on such matters as Tree Root System, Tree Roots and Foundations and Trees in Dispute.

Arboricultural Association
Ampfield House
Romsey
Hampshire SO51 9PA
01794 368717

A professional organization, which produces a directory of approved consultants and contractors.

Australia

Royal Horticultural Society
PO Box 4728
Sydney
NSW 2001
Mr Stephen Anstill

Royal Horticultural Society
PO Box 1921
Brisbane
Queensland 4001
Mr N. Noack

Royal Agricultural and Horticultural Society of South Australia
PO Box 108
Greenwood
South Australia 5034
G T Campbell

Royal Agricultural Society of New South Wales
PO Box 4317
Sydney
NSW 2001
Mr Ranald Moore

Garden Club Australia
50 Lachlan Street
Thirroul
NSW 2515

Australian Garden Horticultural Society
PO Box 972 Bowral
NSW 2576
fax 61 (0) 3 96505043

Canada

Victoria Horticultural Society
PO 5081
Station B
Victoria BC
V8R 6N3
Miss Samantha Ewing

Newfoundland Horticultural Society
728 Main Road
PO Box 84
Goulds
St John
Newfoundland
A1S 1G3
K G Proudfoot

South Africa

Botanical Society of South Africa
Claremont 7795
Capetown
Kirsten Bosch

Transvaal Horticultural Society
9 Walkways
29 Rothesay Avenue
Craighall Park 2196
Johannesburg

Further Reading

General

The RHS Plant Finder 1998/9
Dorling Kindersley 1998

A grand alphabetic listing of which plants (65000 of them) are sold by which nurseries. Always up to date and accurate on Latin names.

The Plant Finder Reference Library CD Rom
John Stockdale Published annually.
Website http://www.plantfinder.co.uk

The electronic version of The Plant Finder book plus much more. The Standard disc includes Seed Search, Fruit and Veg Finder and various reference works. The Professional disc includes the European Plant Finder and Gardening by Mail (USA) etc.

The Gardening Yearbook (Royal Horticultural Society)
Brickell and Joyce
Dorling Kindersley 1996

A well-illustrated manual of seasonal pruning, for ornamentals and fruit trees. Includes major tree pruning, and initial training of young trees.

The Pruning of Trees, Shrubs and Conifers
George E. Brown
Timber Press (USA) 1995
An old stager of a book, but always worthwhile on individual species.

Pests and Diseases

The Royal Horticultural Society: Pests and Diseases
Pippa Greenwood and Andrew Halstead
Dorling Kindersley 1997

An excellent well-illustrated guide to pests and diseases, how to recognise them and how to defeat them. Not afraid to name chemicals.

Diagnosis of Ill-Health in Trees
R.G. Stouts and T.G. Winter
The Stationery Office Books 1994

Useful to consult and lots of pictures of pathological horrors. Not to be looked at by garden hypochondriacs.

Plants

Perennial Garden Plants
Graham Stuart Thomas
J.M. Dent 1993

There are dozens of books on perennials but this is the one you will return to in the end. Few pictures but plenty of information.

The Hillier Manual of Trees and Shrubs
David & Charles 1998

No gardener can do without this encyclopaedic catalogue of trees and shrubs hardy in Britain. Good on varieties as well as species. Few illustrations.

Botanica
Ebury Press 1997

An enormous illustrated encyclopaedia of garden plants, covering plants for the British climate and many for warmer climates also. Saves you buying a separate book on doubtfully hardy plants.

Gardening in Shade
Jane Taylor
J.M. Dent 1991

Excellent on finding plants to grow in all the different kinds of shade, including the difficult kinds like dry, rooty shade.

The Dry Garden
Beth Chatto
J.M. Dent 1978

A modern classic, and just the thing when choosing perennials for dry soils. Sound as a rock, but one longs for her to publish a revised version.

Plants for Dry Gardens
Jane Taylor
Frances Lincoln 1993

A fine source of information on plants for dry gardens in warmer or Mediterranean climates.

Inspirational

The Wild Garden
William Robinson
Timber Press (USA) 1994 out of print

Still one of the best books on which plants naturalise well and will withstand life in the rough. A good provocative read.

Perennials and their Garden Habitats
R. Hansen and F. Stahl
Cambridge University Press 1993

Translated from the German, this is the bible of eco-gardeners wanting to do modern things with massed perennials. Useful on plant communities for different habitats.

Plants in Garden History
Penelope Hobhouse
Pavilion 1992

An invaluable and thorough journey through garden history, with plenty of illustrations of period garden style as well as the plants themselves.

The Essential Garden Book
Terence Conran and Dan Pearson
Conran Octopus 1998

Something to brighten up your ideas. A source of modernist inspiration for those who want to get out of the mixed-border Gertrude Jekyll rut.

Creating a Garden
Mary Keen
Conran Octopus 1996

Generous words of practical and design wisdom from someone who is rejuvenating as much as creating a garden.

The Gardener's Year
Karel Capek
1929 out of print

The best gardening book ever. It will never fail to make you smile when things go wrong. It will rejuvenate you.

Harvesting the Edge
Geoffrey Dutton
Menard Press 1995

If ever you wonder if you are doing too much too fast, read Geoffrey Dutton. He will teach you, as no one else can, to stop and look at your garden, to learn from it and enjoy it.

Index

NOTE *Page numbers in italic refer to illustrations or their captions.*

Picture Acknowledgements

1: GPL/Tim Griffiths; 2–3: GPL/John Bouchier; 8 GPL/Brigitte Thomas; 12: GPL/Lamontagne; 13: top left: GPL/Jane Legate; top right: GPL/JS Sira; bottom left & right: Nic Barlow; 14: GPL/Brigitte Thomas; 15: top left: GPL/Anne Kelley; bottom right: GPL/Brigitte Thomas; 16: GPL/Nigel Francis; 17: GPL/Howard Rice; inset: GPL/Jane Legate; 18–19: GPL/Brigitte Thomas; 20: Hugh Palmer; 21: bottom left: Stephen Anderton; top right: GPL/JS Sira; 22: top left and bottom right: GPL/Lamontagne; 23: top: GPL/Ron Evans; bottom: GPL/John Glover; 24: GPL/Ron Sutherland; 25: top left and centre: GPL/John Glover; top right: GPL/Sunniva Harte; bottom left: Nic Barlow; 26: top left and right: Nic Barlow; bottom right: Stephen Anderton; 27: GPL/RobertEstall; 28: GPL/Kate Zari Roberts; 29: bottom left: Stephen Anderton; top right: GPL/Dennis Davis; 30: bottom left (before and after) Stephen Anderton; top right: GPL/Ron Sutherland; 31: GPL/Kate Zari Roberts; 32: GPL/Kate Zari Roberts; 33: bottom left: GPL/Kate Zari Roberts; top right: GPL/Ron Sutherland; 34: GPL/Clay Perry; 35: Stephen Anderton; 36: GPL/Bob Challinor; 37: top left: GPL/Juliette Wade; bottom right: GPL/Ron Evans; 38: GPL/Mel Watson; 39: bottom left and top right: GPL/Ron Evans; 40: top: GPL/Lamontagne; bottom: GPL/Marijke Heuff; 41: top: GPL/Clive Boursnell; bottom: GPL/Brigitte Thomas; 42–43: Stephen Anderton; 46: GPL/JS Sira; 47: top left: GPL/Brigitte Thomas; bottom right: GPL/Mayer/Le Scanff; 48: GPL/Janet Sorrell; 49: top left: GPL/Howard Rice; bottom right: GPL/David England; 50: left: Hugh Palmer; right: GPL/David Askham; 51: top: GPL/Lamontagne; bottom left and right: GPL/Lynne Brotchie; 52: left and right: GPL/Steven Wooster; 53: GPL/Ron Sutherland; 54: GPL/Henk Dijkman; 55: GPL/Jane Legate; 56: bottom left: GPL/Brian Carter; top right: Stephen Anderton; 57: bottom left and top right: Stephen Anderton; 58: GPL/Mayer/Le Scanff; 59: top: GPL/Neil Holmes; bottom left: GPL/Ann Kelley; bottom right: GPL/John Glover; 60: GPL/Lamontagne; 61: bottom left: GPL/Lamontagne; top right: GPL/Jacqui Hurst; 62–63: GPL/John Miller; 64: GPL/Ann Kelley; 65: top left: GPL/Mel Watson; bottom right: GPL/Brigitte Thomas; 66: Stephen Anderton; 67: Nic Barlow; 68: centre left: GPL/David England; top right: Nic Barlow; 69: Nic Barlow; 70: GPL/Geoff Dann; 71: GPL/David England; 72: bottom left: GPL/Brian Carter; top right: GPL/Lynne Brotchie; 73: GPL/Steven Wooster; 74: Forest Research Photo Library; 75: top left: GPL/Lamontagne; bottom right: GPL/Erika Craddock; 76–77: Marijke Heuff; inset: GPL/Howard Rice; 78: Stephen Anderton; 79: top: GPL/Zara McCalmont; bottom left and right: Howard Rice; 80: bottom left: GPL/Robert Estall; top right: GPL/Lamontagne; 81: GPL/Marijke Heuff; 82: bottom left: GPL/Andrea Jones; top right: GPL/Steven Wooster; 83: top left: Nic Barlow; top right: GPL/John Glover; bottom GPL/Michael Howes; 84: GPL/John Glover; 85: bottom left: GPL/Jon Bouchier; top right: GPL/Howard Rice; 86: bottom left: GPL/Jane Legate; top right: GPL/John Glover; 87: top: GPL/Bob Challinor; bottom: GPL/Lamontagne; 88: top GPL/John Glover; bottom: GPL/Neil Holmes; 89: left: GPL/David England; right: GPL/Michael Howes; 91: GPL/Christopher Gallagher; 92:–96: Michelle Garrett; 97: left: GPL/John Glover; centre: GPL/Marie O'Hara; 98: left: GPL/JS Sira; centre: GPL/John Glover; right: GPL/Michel Viard; 99: left: GPL/Neil Holmes; centre: GPL/Jerry Pavia; 100: left: GPL/Linda Burgess; right: GPL/Ron Evans; 101: left: GPL/John Glover; centre: GPL/Brian Carter; right: GPL/David Askham; 102: left: GPL/Nick Meers; inset: Stephen Anderton; right: GPL/Jacqui Hurst; 103: left: GPL/Brigitte Thomas; centre: GPL/JS Sira; 104: left: GPL/Brigitte Thomas; centre: GPL/Christopher Fairweather; right: GPL/John Glover; 105: left: Zara McCalmont; right: GPL/JS Sira; 106: left: GPL/Christopher Fairweather; centre: GPL/Sunniva Harte; right: GPL/Howard Rice; 107: left: GPL/Steven Wooster; centre and right: GPL/JS Sira; 108: left: GPL/John Glover; centre: GPL/Juliette Wade; right: GPL/Didier Willey; 109: left: GPL/John Glover; right: GPL/Lamontagne; 110: left: GPL/John Glover; centre: GPL/Christopher Gallagher; right: GPL/JS Sira; 111: left: GPL/JS Sira; right: GPL/Kathy Charlton; 112: left: GPL/Howard Rice; centre: GPL/Clive Nichols; right: GPL/Steven Wooster; 113: left: GPL/Zara McCalmont; centre: GPL/Brian Carter; right: GPL/JS Sira; 114: left: GPL/Brigitte Thomas; centre: GPL/JS Sira; right: GPL/John Glover; 115: left: GPL/Nigel Temple; right: GPL/Neil Holmes; 116: left: GPL/Lamontagne; centre: GPL/Ron Evans; right: GPL/Howard Rice; 117: left: GPL/John Glover; centre; GPL/Neil Holmes; right: GPL/Brian Carter; 118: centre: GPL/JS Sira; right: GPL/John Glover; 119: left and right: GPL/JS Sira; 120: centre top: GPL/Sunniva Harte; centre bottom: GPL/Lamontagne; 121: left: GPL/John Glover; centre top: GPL/JS Sira; centre bottom: GPL/Didier Willery; 122: left: GPL/Vaughan Fleming; right: Stephen Anderton; 123: left and centre: GPL/Brian Carter; right: GPL/Didier Willery; 124: left: GPL/Steven Wooster; centre: GPL/Linda Burgess; 125: left: GPL/Howard Rice; centre: GPL/Sunniva Harte; right: GPL/John Glover; 126: top: GPL/Neil Holmes; bottom left to right: GPL/John Glover; GPL/John Glover; GPL/Christopher Gallagher; GPL/Brian Carter; 127: left: GPL/Brian Carter; centre: GPL/Phillipe Bonduel; right: GPL/Vivian Russel; 128: left: GPL/JS Sira; inset: GPL/John Glover; right: GPL/Densey Cline; 129: left: GPL/Christopher Gallagher; centre: GPL/Mayer/Le Scanff; 130: left: GPL/Bob Challinor; right: GPL/Christopher Fairweather; 131: left: GPL/Howard Rice; centre; GPL/Brian Carter; right: GPL/Christopher Fairweather; 132: left: GPL/JS Sira; centre; GPL/Howard Rice; 133: left: GPL/John Glover; centre: GPL/Clive Boursnell; right: GPL/Neil Holmes; 134: left: GPL/Brian Carter; centre: GPL/John Glover; left: GPL/Christopher Gallagher; 135: left: GPL/Howard Rice; centre and right: GPL/John Glover; 136: left: GPL/Lynne Brotchie; centre: GPL/JS Sira; 137: GPL/Linda Burgess; right: GPL/John Glover; 138: left: GPL/Brigitte Thomas; centre: GPL/Gary Rogers; left: GPL/Henk Dijkman; 139: left: GPL/Joanne Pavia; top right: GPL/Dennis Davis; bottom right: GPL/John Glover; 140: GPL/John Glover; 141: top left and bottom: Stephen Anderton; top right: GPL/Lamontagne; 142: top left: Stephen Anderton; bottom left: GPL/John McCarthy; 143: left: GPL/David Askham; right: GPL/G.Dalton; 144: left: GPL/Brian Carter; top right: GPL/John Glover; bottom right: GPL/Jacqui Hurst; 145; left: GPL/Brigitte Thomas; top right: GPL/JS Sira; bottom right: GPL/Lamontagne; 146–147: GPL